The Armenian Genocide

A Captivating Guide to the Massacre of the Armenians by the Turks of the Ottoman Empire

Free Bonus from Captivating History (Available for a Limited time)

Hi History Lovers!

Now you have a chance to join our exclusive history list so you can get your first history ebook for free as well as discounts and a potential to get more history books for free! Simply visit the link below to join.

Captivatinghistory.com/ebook

Also, make sure to follow us on Facebook, Twitter and Youtube by searching for Captivating History.

Contents

Introduction

"Eat up! Think of the poor starving children in Armenia."

These words, commonly spoken in American households one hundred years ago, sound strange and foreign today. In fact, many of us might not even know where Armenia is. But during the horrors of the First World War, arguably no nation suffered as desperately as Armenia did.

The persecution of the Jewish during the Second World War, known worldwide as the Holocaust, is still very much present in global memory; a fact perhaps in part made possible by the widespread recognition that Germany recognizes its past mistakes. While politicians and civilians alike commemorate the deaths of roughly six million Jews from 1933 to 1945, the world has begun to forget a genocide that occurred twenty years before WWII started. And part of that may be because the nation that perpetrated it—modern-day Turkey—refuses to acknowledge that the genocide happened at all.

During 1915 to 1923, one and a half million Armenian people were deported and killed in the most appalling ways comprehensible. They were ripped from their homes (in a land where they had lived for longer than history can tell, a land so old that many speculate it was the site of the biblical Garden of Eden) and sent off on death marches across the blistering Syrian Desert. They were shot on the thresholds of the houses where they were raising their children. They were butchered with swords in gruesome ways in order to dishearten those left alive. They were starved in concentration camps, they were burned and drowned and beaten to death by the thousands, and then their corpses were stripped naked and left to rot in the open air. They were overdosed with morphine. They were injected with infected blood. They were cast overboard into the frigid Black Sea. They were gassed. They were raped. They were abducted and sold as slaves.

In short, the Ottoman Empire under the Three Pashas made every possible attempt to exterminate the Armenian race with such fervor that their actions would inspire the creation of the very word that now defines the greatest crime that can be perpetrated against a civilization: genocide. Yet today, the Armenian Genocide is an event that has melted out of the collective consciousness. It is an event that has repercussions extending to the modern day and is an event that should never be forgotten.

Do you know about the Armenians? Do you really know? Let this book show you, walking in the footsteps of the Armenian people starting in ancient times when they became the first officially Christian nation and started a precedent of having a strong national identity. Let it walk you through the oppressed lives of the Armenians during the Ottoman Empire. Let it stand you in their shoes as the first wave of genocide hits them. Let it make you a witness to their terrible suffering.

And let it give you hope. For the Armenians died, and they suffered, and they were mistreated in a way that can hardly be comprehended, but they did one thing more than anything else.

They survived.

Chapter 1 – The Armenian Problem

The ancient scriptures tell the story of Noah, an old man who believed passionately in a god who'd been forgotten by the rest of the world. As the world was plunged into sin and darkness, Noah and his family alone listened for the light. When he was told that the world would be purged by means of a great and deadly flood, Noah knew that he alone would be spared but only if he built an ark: a gigantic wooden ship in which he and his family could shelter through the coming storm. And so, famously, Noah and his family boarded the ark alongside two of each kind of animal, and then it began to rain.

When the forty days and forty nights of rain had ceased, the earth was covered in water, the ark helplessly afloat on a flooded world. Noah and his family would drift for days until, at last, the ark ran aground. When the water finally cleared, they discovered that they had landed on the summit of a great mountain: Mount Ararat.

Today, Mount Ararat overlooks the sprawling city of Yerevan, the capital of Armenia—one of the oldest civilizations in the world. The genocide that would take place in the very shadow of the revered mountain is a terrible bloodstain on the face of a long and illustrious history that dates back many thousands of years.

* * * *

Modern-day Armenia is a small, landlocked country bordered by Turkey, Georgia, Azerbaijan, and Iran. Its towering mountains and deep valleys, cut from the landscape by swift-flowing rivers, have been the setting for millennia of human history.

People have been living in Armenia for so long that some traditions have identified it as the location of the biblical Garden of Eden, and science has discovered evidence of the most ancient human civilizations within its borders. Armenic Sumerian records dating back more than four thousand years suggests that Armenia may have been the first home of humanity.

The ancient land of Armenia was far larger than its modern-day equivalent. Encompassing much of its modern-day neighbors, ancient Armenia was a target for the Persians. Armenians are first mentioned by that name in Greek texts from around the 7th century BCE. Its scattered tribes were conquered under Alexander the Great in 331. It rose to prominence around the 1st century BCE when it was ruled by arguably its greatest king, Tigranes II. However, shortly after Tigranes' reign ended in 55 BCE, it was conquered again—this time by the greatest power of the ancient world: Rome.

Rome would continue to rule Armenia for centuries, although it had its own king and was relatively independent of the old, great empire, apart from it being used as a battlefield in Rome's continual struggles with the Parthians, who were from modern-day Iran. In fact, it was a Parthian king that would briefly overthrow the Romans in 53 CE, prompting a struggle over Armenian territory until a Roman emperor, Nero, made peace by crowning the Parthian leader—Tiridates I—king of Armenia, but he would also be a vassal to Rome.

It was Tiridates III, a descendant of Tiridates I, who would change the course of Armenian history. Its tribes would be united under one faith, a new and strange faith that was spreading like wildfire on the bare feet of its disciples throughout the ancient world. Little did he know what repercussions this simple act would have on the history of his people in a little less than two thousand years.

* * * *

For centuries, Armenian tribes had practiced polytheism, like many of the other ancient peoples surrounding them—including the Romans, who had been Armenia's ruler and strongest ally for hundreds of years by the end of the 3rd century CE. Yet ever since the ancient apostle Paul had come to Antioch, rumors of a new faith had been spreading throughout the land. This faith was Christianity, and it was still in its very infancy, yet it captured the hearts of the Armenians.

By this point, Armenia was being ruled by Tiridates III but only with the help of Diocletian, the Roman emperor. The Persians had invaded and seized Armenia, assassinating Tiridates' father in the process, and only the imperial army had been able to drive them out and place Tiridates III on his rightful throne. He had formed a powerful alliance with Diocletian, and the two were on good terms.

He was not on good terms, however, with the noble families that had been involved in his father's assassination. These families faced punishment for the conspiracy, except for one young member: Grigor, known in English history as Gregory.

The story of St. Gregory the Illuminator is so old that it is part history and part tradition, but the version that follows is largely taken from a contemporary history by Agathangelos. The tale tells how his nurse, a Christian lady, had carried him off to safety as a mere baby and raised him as her own. When Tiridates III retook the throne, Gregory was consumed with guilt for what his father had done. He was driven by a desire to atone for his father's sins, and he hoped to do so by bringing what he perceived to be the greatest gift of all to the country his father had betrayed: the Christian faith.

Joining Tiridates' court, Gregory quickly discovered that this would not be as easy as he'd hoped. Like the majority of the country,

Tiridates was a pagan, and he expected his court to worship the same gods as he did. When Gregory refused to bow down to Tiridates' gods, the king was outraged that a mere palace functionary would dare to defy his king. He had Gregory tortured and then hurled into the deep, dark prison of Khor Virap, which means "pit of oblivion." Nobody ever came back from that dank pit, which stood in the very shadow of Mount Ararat.

Enraged, Tiridates—right alongside Diocletian—launched a series of persecutions against the Christians in his realm. However, soon, he would have bigger and more personal problems to deal with. Shortly after Gregory's imprisonment, Tiridates began to experience a series of extremely strange symptoms. While often perfectly lucid, he would occasionally be overcome with strange fits where he would behave, according to tradition, like a wild boar. It became frighteningly obvious to his subjects that the king was losing his mind. For twelve long years, Gregory languished in Khor Virap, and Tiridates continued to go more and more insane.

It was Tiridates' sister, Khosrovidukht, who turned out to be a lifeline for both Tiridates and his forgotten prisoner. She experienced a vision that only Gregory would be able to cure her brother, and in desperation, she went to Khor Virap to find him. Surprised to discover that he was still alive after twelve years, Khosrovidukht brought Gregory to the raving Tiridates' bedside. Gregory laid his hands on the stricken king and prayed for him to be healed, and the king awoke from his madness, never to have it return again.

So goes Armenian tradition for the reason why Tiridates did what he did next, but history has little doubt of the actions that followed. After he converted to Christianity himself, Tiridates not only stopped persecuting Christians in his domain, but in 301 CE, he also made Christianity the official religion of Armenia. Thus, according to Armenians, it became the first country to officially adopt Christianity as its state religion. And for the next thirteen centuries, the Armenian people would cling to this faith—even though a time would come when it would cost them more dearly than they could have ever expected.

* * * *

As the years passed, the Armenian people continued to prove that they were nothing if not different from everyone else, and they were unafraid to defend their individualism from the rest of the world.

The Sassanid dynasty of the Persian Empire was the next to attempt to overwhelm Armenia in 451 under Yazdegerd II. The Sassanids followed the Zoroastrian religion and unwisely attempted to forcibly convert the Armenians to their religion. The Armenians fought back so strenuously that even the powerful Sassanids were unable to conquer them spiritually, even though they had more success militarily.

For the next two hundred years, Armenia continued to keep its religion stubbornly independent from the encroaching empires—the Persian and the Byzantine Empires—that were attempting to assimilate it. In 634, an Arab invasion resulted in decades of war and then centuries of captivity by the Arabian caliphate of the time. It was only in the late 9th century that Armenia would regain its independence and move forward into the Middle Ages as its own realm, still clinging to Christianity as its state religion. Thus, Armenia supported the European crusaders, proving itself by playing a key role in providing a safe refuge for crusading armies en route to the Holy Land.

When Armenia itself came under attack from Egyptian Mamluks in the 14th century, however, the European powers that had been so quick to use Armenia in its crusades were nowhere to be seen. In fact, for the next several centuries, Armenia would be under constant attack from a variety of Muslim powers. One of these would prove to be Armenia's greatest nemesis and the enemy that would commit the greatest atrocity of them all against the Armenian people: The Ottoman Empire.

Chapter 2 – The Ottoman Empire

Illustration I: A 19ᵗʰ-century depiction of Mehmed the Conqueror entering Constantinople

Trampling upon the ashes of the Byzantine Empire rose a new superpower, one that

would prove to last for centuries and control much of Europe and Asia: The Ottoman Empire.

The empire was named after its founder, Osman I, a Turkish tribal leader who lived in the late 13th century. Osman was ambitious and ready for more power than simply leading a few tribes in Anatolia, and he and his successors started to carve out a powerful Islamic empire throughout the next two hundred years.

Osman and his successors had little difficulty finding support for their military campaigns. Ever since its rise around the 7th century CE, Islam had spread like wildfire throughout the Middle East, Europe, Asia, and North Africa, and for many Muslims, that meant joining the jihad: an ongoing holy war against all non-Muslims. The jihad was not unlike the crusades, which had been undertaken by the Roman Catholic Church in the Middle Ages. Unlike the ill-fated crusades, however, the jihad would be both enduring and militarily successful, fueled by a belief in its followers that non-Muslims had to be conquered.

With thousands of young people filled with a religious zeal for war, military leaders—who were hungry not just for perceived holiness but also for land and power—were able to amass enormous armies for campaigns all over the world. As the Ottoman Empire grew to engulf Turkey and parts of the Middle East, its greatest rival proved to be the eastern relic of the ancient Roman Empire: The Byzantine Empire. Having been founded on the bedrock of the Eastern Orthodox Church, the Byzantine Empire and Christianity were inextricably linked. That made it a target for the profoundly Islamic Ottoman Empire—and so did its considerable lands and riches, which held tremendous appeal for the rulers of the Ottoman Empire, who were determined to expand their borders and amass power and wealth for their dominion.

The Byzantine Empire, which had been in existence since 330 CE, was in decline by the 15th century but nonetheless remained an important power of Christian Europe. Its capital, Constantinople, had long been a jewel of Eastern Europe as a center of power, commerce, government, and culture. And it was Constantinople that the Ottoman rulers—known as sultans—really wanted. To topple Constantinople would be to destroy the Byzantine Empire, and destroying the Byzantine Empire would not only bring huge lands and wealth to the Ottoman Empire, but it would also break down the great wall that stood between the Ottomans and the lushness of Western Europe.

Tamerlane, the terrifying ruler and founder of the Timurid Empire, was the only leader who was able to hold back the Ottoman Empire for long. During the brief and glorious existence of his empire, this Asian conqueror crushed the Ottoman Empire and prevented it from going through his domain to reach the Byzantine Empire. However, Tamerlane's empire would not last long. After his death in 1405, it crumbled to nothing, and the way was clear for the Ottoman Empire to charge through and meet its single greatest foe.

And its sultan, Mehmed II—known to history as Mehmed the Conqueror—was the man for the job.

* * * *

Mehmed was only twenty years old when he led his army to the very walls of Constantinople, but he was nonetheless an accomplished general.

Mehmed had only been the sultan for two years when he began the siege that would earn him the title of "Mehmed the Conqueror," and he had spent much of that time preparing to besiege Constantinople. Once the greatest city of Eastern Europe, the decline of the Byzantine Empire had robbed the city of the glory it had possessed at its very height, but it was still no small challenge that lay before the young sultan, who was determined to wipe Christianity out of the Byzantine Empire—and, of course, amass those considerable lands for himself. Yet it was still evident that Mehmed had one tremendous advantage: sheer numbers. Constantinople's troops, led by Emperor Constantine XI, numbered only about eight thousand. The Ottomans, on the other hand, came in a great wave of men more than ten times that number.

As was typical of Ottoman sultans, Mehmed invested heavily and focused on warfare, and no siege would be as expensive as that of Constantinople. He built fortresses near the city specifically for the battle and commissioned enormous cannons to be built in order to batter down Constantinople's walls. Outnumbered though the Byzantines were, they had the great advantage of the ancient city's vast defenses. The men inside were few, but their fortress was still one of the most defensible in Europe.

No number of walls or defenses were going to deter Mehmed, however. Cutting off routes for reinforcements to enter the city by either land or sea, he began the siege on April 6th, 1453.

The days that followed, according to historical tradition, were the last 53 days of the Middle Ages. They were long and arduous, not only for the beleaguered Byzantines but also for Mehmed's own men. Viewing many of his own troops as expendable, Mehmed sent them forward in waves upon waves to batter themselves to death against Constantinople's staunch walls. While it was a ruthless choice, it was an effective one; the Ottomans succeeded in systematically breaking down more and more of Constantinople's defenses. Yet somehow, the city clung on, with Emperor Constantine knowing that his city was the last bastion between the Ottomans and the rest of Christendom. For almost two months, the city stood firm against the onslaught.

On the eve of May 26th, Mehmed withdrew his troops. What the Byzantines must have hoped to be a retreat, however, was simply the calm before the storm. Mehmed wasn't giving up—he was preparing for one last great charge, one final bid to bring Constantinople to its knees.

Abandoned by Western European kings, Emperor Constantine's only reinforcements came from a handful of volunteers who had come to Constantinople on their own accord. His repeated pleas for help from the surrounding kings had fallen upon deaf ears. The Byzantine Empire's western counterpart, the Holy Roman Empire, had itself declined in power and was occupied with reformation and struggle within its borders; France and England were decimated after a century of war. No one was coming to Constantine's aid, and he had already lost thousands of his soldiers.

It was with only a handful of men that Constantine waited in the dark city as Mehmed's enormous army, numbering more than 100,000 men, rose in the night like a great bear awakening from its brief hibernation. Mehmed and his men had spent 36 hours in rest and prayer, and now they were ready for the conquest. As midnight approached on May 28th, Mehmed sent forward a batch of cannon fodder: his Christian recruits and poorly equipped infantry. They charged the weakened walls, their aim not to overthrow the enemy but to simply tire the outnumbered Byzantines.

It worked. By the time Mehmed's more seasoned soldiers joined the fray, the Byzantine defenses were buckling. First their general and then their emperor attempted to rally the men but were cut down; panic spread through the troops, with some of them abandoning the battle to rush into the city and protect their families, others fleeing to their ships in a desperate bid to get away. Many, knowing what was coming, knowing that Mehmed would take no prisoners, chose to die on their own terms instead. They climbed the walls of Constantinople, reached the battlements, and flung themselves into the air to be dashed to pieces on the rocks below or swallowed up by the sea.

Those that remained in the city would witness utter devastation. Mehmed had promised to give his soldiers three days of free rein to do as they would with the city they had worked so hard to besiege, and those three days of plundering were almost more horrible than the massive slaughter of May 29th. Women were raped and enslaved, and Ottomans fought with one another over the spoils of war. Any who stood against them were butchered without mercy.

Constantinople had fallen, and the triumphant Mehmed had made his name known as a formidable conqueror. It was not without cost to the Ottomans, however. The Byzantine army had lost half its men; the number of Ottoman casualties is unknown, but according to one eyewitness, it was so vast that the gutters of the city ran scarlet with blood.

Despite the cost, Mehmed had gotten exactly what he wanted. Mehmed made Constantinople the capital of his growing empire, and it remains the capital of Turkey to this day, officially known as Istanbul since 1930. With that, the Byzantine Empire was gone. The time had come for a new and great power, the Ottoman Empire, which would last for hundreds of years. And the fall of Constantinople, gruesome as it was, would not be the bloodiest day in its history.

* * * *

It was during the 15th century, at the same time as Mehmed and his successors were conquering the Byzantine Empire, that Armenia, too, would fall before the might of the Ottoman Empire, just as many surrounding countries did.

The incorporation of Armenia into the Ottoman Empire was not as sudden and dramatic as the fall of the Byzantine Empire. Instead, it happened slowly and gradually as the prospering Ottomans started to settle in Armenia. As the Ottoman Empire clashed over and over with Persia, Armenia found itself once again to be the battleground of a war in which it had no part, and its people were thrown from one government to the other. By the 15th century, actual Armenians comprised only one-quarter of the population of their home country; the Persians were gone, and the Ottoman Empire controlled the whole of Armenia.

The growing Ottoman Empire, although its rulers were devoted Muslims, was not entirely Islamic. Religious minorities, such as Jews and various sects of Christianity, were allowed to exist within its borders. Determined to cling on to the faith they'd held for centuries, the majority of Armenians remained Christian, whether they were Catholic, Orthodox, or even Protestant, as the wake of the Reformation and Renaissance had brought change across the globe. Most Armenians, however, clung to the Orthodox Church, an ancient church founded by two of Jesus' original disciples. Thus, even though Armenians were living right alongside their Turkish counterparts, they remained a very distinct people. They worshiped differently. They spoke a different language. They had different ideals and a whole separate culture, and this made them, in the eyes of the Turks, less than human.

By the late 18th century, the Ottoman Empire had started to decline. The brilliance that it had reached in the 16th century under the wise rule of Suleiman the Magnificent had started to wear off, and pressure was mounting from the rest of Europe as power shifted and changed around the world. The French Revolution, the Napoleonic Wars, and the end of the Western Holy Roman Empire had made seismic shifts in the power of the world; the Middle East had torn itself from the Ottoman grip, and the once-mighty empire was now struggling to control what was left of its lands.

The decline of Ottoman power was a boon for the Armenians. Their small population was still hanging on and managing to prosper despite oppression from their Turkish government. Still allowed to practice their faith, the Armenians were subject to harsh treatment as being inferior and second-class, and they were known as infidels by the Turks. They were also taxed more harshly than their Muslim neighbors. Nonetheless, the struggling empire was forced to put some reforms into place, and this allowed the Armenians to occupy important positions, even in the government itself.

None of this changed the fact that the Armenians still held on to their religion, their language, and their culture. Their strong national identity never wavered, despite their integration into the Ottoman Empire, and for a time in the mid-18th century, it looked as though they would be allowed to flourish even though they were different.

Nothing could have been further from the truth.

Chapter 3 – The First Massacres

The struggling Ottoman Empire, already limping and licking its wounds after losing many of its lands, was facing increasing pressure from the rest of the world—and this time, the European powers were not seeking to seize Ottoman lands. Instead, they had taken issue with the very philosophies upon which the Ottoman government was founded.

Ever since the Protestant Reformation in the early 16th century, Europe had been wrestling with the question of religious freedom. Wars broke out all over the continent as Christian powers faced a great rift within their own countries, and it took centuries to move toward tolerance and religious freedom. But by the 18th century, the question had started to settle somewhat. Most countries were at least allowing Protestants to practice in peace, and religious diversity was becoming more common. And it was soon brought to Europe's attention that the Ottoman Empire was late to the party. After the Congress of Berlin finished in July 1878, the subject of the treatment of Armenians by the Ottoman government had become known as the "Armenian question." The rest of Europe was placing increasing pressure on the Ottoman Empire to reform their treatment of Armenians and other religious and ethnic minorities, and as tensions began to erupt across the continent, the Ottoman Empire pushed back against the pressure.

The Ottoman government's reluctance to treat its minorities better was not solely founded on religion. Instead, Russia—a long-time enemy of the empire—was one of the greatest motivators. Having been a Christian nation for centuries, Russia was not only a military threat but also a religious one. It was feared that Armenians would become more loyal to the Christian government of Russia than the Islamic one of the Ottoman Empire, and considering that there were over one million Armenian people in the empire at the time, this could have been disastrous.

No one feared Russia more than Abdul Hamid II. And his fear and greed would turn out to be a terrible curse for the Armenians because he was their sultan.

* * * *

Abdul Hamid II was born in 1842 to Sultan Abdulmejid, the last in a long line of sultans that had wielded absolute power over their empire. His father enjoyed unrivaled power, and even though Abdul Hamid's mother died when he was a boy, his father—who was a polygamist, like many Ottoman sultans—was still able to provide him with a fairly structured family environment. He was adopted by one of his father's other wives and was able to explore his interests as an adolescent and young man, most notably carpentry and the opera. In fact, Abdul Hamid would be one of the first to translate opera classics into Turkish. In the summer of 1867, when Abdul Hamid was a young man in his twenties, his uncle took him to tour the rest of the world. This was a rare activity for a young prince of the empire, but he was able to accompany his uncle to cities like London and Paris.

After the deposition of Abdul Hamid's older brother, he ascended to the throne in 1876, and many of his subjects thought he would support the rising liberal movement within the empire. It was not only the rest of Europe that was crying out for Ottoman reformation, but also many of its subjects—both minorities and Muslims—wanted change. But Abdul Hamid would do no such thing. When he inherited the empire, it was already on the very brink of disaster. Russia was threatening war, and Abdul Hamid had only been sultan for a year when war was declared.

It lasted only a year. The Ottoman Empire, once the power that had toppled Constantinople, was a shadow of its former self; it stood no chance against the angry behemoth that was Russia (which had also allied with Great Britain). The Congress of Berlin—which made the term "Armenian question" popular in the media—negotiated peace in 1878 after Ottoman defeat.

All across Europe, trouble continued to brew. It became obvious to Abdul Hamid that he would have to find a powerful ally to stand alongside him, and he started to take steps to secure a friendship with Germany. Relations with Russia were still very rocky, especially considering that there was tension between Britain and Germany, and this was only made worse when the Armenians began to look toward their Christian neighbor with longing. In the Ottoman Empire's weakened state, it could not afford to deal with an Armenian rebellion. This could likely have been avoided by providing the Armenians with fairer treatment, but Abdul Hamid was not interested in doing so. He clung to the ways of his forefathers even as the empire they built was crumbling around him.

While the Congress of Berlin had required the Ottoman Empire to reform its policies toward the Armenians, ultimately, Abdul Hamid never complied. Instead, he started to oppress the Armenians even more than before. In response, two Armenian revolutionary parties were formed. Most of the Armenians didn't support these parties, except for a handful of rebels, but they caused widespread panic throughout Abdul Hamid's administration. Abdul Hamid would insult them by calling them cowards and a terrible threat. Even as the ruins of his empire began to fall down around his ears, he refused to see any fault of his own, instead blaming Christian Europe for his troubles and considering the Armenians to be a dangerous group that might "tear out our very guts."

Asked by a journalist about the Armenian question in 1890, Abdul Hamid's words were dark and frightening. "I will soon settle those Armenians."

And in 1894, he attempted to do so. A group of Kurdish brigands had been causing chaos in his empire, and he made no attempt to stop them from wreaking havoc. Instead, he armed them and gave them a focus: they were to make Armenian lives as difficult as possible, and whatever they did, it would be considered legal. These men became known as the Hamidian Regiment, or the *Hamidiye*, and they were quick to exploit the free rein that their sultan had given them. Driving off rural Armenians' livestock, they plundered their homes, raped their women, and butchered those who would dare to stand against them.

The death toll began to rise, and the greater powers of Europe—France, Great Britain, and Russia—decided that something needed to be done. Clearly, the Congress of Berlin had done nothing to curb Abdul Hamid's harsh treatment of the Armenians, and the *Hamidiye* were proof of that. A reform package was sent to him in 1895, demanding that he stop the rampage of his renegade soldiers at once and start implementing the reforms he had promised back in 1878. Abdul Hamid received the package with typical stubbornness. "This business will end in blood," he said darkly.

And it did. Hearing of the reform package, thousands of Armenians gathered in Constantinople to show their support of the reforms and demanded that they be implemented. For some of them, October 1st, 1895, would be their last day. When the rally began to get loud and angry as the people petitioned for a better life, Turkish policemen were sent in to break it up. Instead of bringing help to the Armenians, the reforms had already brought nothing but even more violence.

It was nothing compared to the atrocities that would follow.

* * * *

Susan Wheeler had come to the Ottoman Empire to minister to a people oppressed by hatred. She hadn't expected to flee for her life.

The Armenian question was a European concern, but it was a topic that spread like wildfire throughout the United States. Children were told to finish their dinner no longer because of the "starving children in Africa," but because of the "starving children in Armenia." Armenians became the cause of the day, and many wealthy Americans donated to the Red Cross and other organizations that were trying to help the people there. Yet for some Americans, simply raising awareness or funds was simply not enough. Some of them felt convicted to go to Armenia themselves, and Susan and her husband, Reverend Crosby Howard Wheeler, were among them.

In their book "A Bouquet from Our Missionary Garden," Susan and Crosby would tell the story of how they traveled to Harput, Turkey, in order to support the Armenian Christians in their persecution, decades before the massacres started. They set up a mission station to provide a place of worship as well as schools for Christian children, and as news of massacres in Constantinople and other areas of Turkey began to reach them, they knew that trouble was coming. But like many Protestant American missionaries, the Wheelers refused to flee back to a home country where there was both peace and freedom. Instead, they held firm and waited for the *Hamidiye* to descend upon Harput.

The officials in the city had promised to protect the Armenians from the *Hamidiye*, and when the first of the frightening Kurds began to seep out of the mountains—the regiment streaming down onto the plain like rivers of blood—Harput's cannons were made ready to fire. Terrified, Armenians poured into the mission station, desperate for refuge; none were turned away, although Crosby, at this point, was wheelchair-bound. Susan and her helpers watched and prayed as the *Hamidiye* swept toward the city while the cannons were being loaded. The city would protect them. The city had said it would.

The city had lied. When the great crack of the cannon rang through the air and the smell of gunpowder unleashed battle on the senses, the ammunition was not launched toward the marauding *Hamidiye*. Instead, the cannons were firing on the Armenian quarter of the city itself. The Harput defenses would not be doing any defending against the *Hamidiye*—instead, Susan had to watch, appalled, as the Armenians' own home city was turned against them. Death rained down upon their homes, and when the *Hamidiye* burst into the city itself, matters were made much worse. They were bent not only on massacring the people but also on destroying their homes.

Susan and her companions fled from one missionary building to the other, pausing to stare out of the windows as flames sprang up throughout the city in the falling darkness. Smoke rose above Harput, leaving the Muslim Turks' homes untouched; the Armenians were the target, and they would be shown no mercy. Fearing for their lives, Armenians and missionaries alike were forced to flee the schools and churches where they were seeking refuge, heading for the newest building that the Wheelers had worked tirelessly to erect. It was the library, but getting there would not be easy. Susan was aging herself; Crosby would have to be carried, and in the utter pandemonium, she had no idea how this could be done.

Crosby's salvation came from an unlikely quarter: a group of Kurdish people, just like the *Hamidiye*. But while these young men shared the same ethnicity with the murderers plundering the city, they had been Crosby's students, and they refused to join their kinfolk's rampage. Instead, they scooped Crosby into a rocking chair and carried him to the library, hundreds of missionaries and Armenians hot on their heels.

Hidden away in the library, defended by a few brave volunteers in a fire engine, Susan, Crosby, and their friends watched as the Christian part of the city burned around them. Men, women, and children were butchered by the *Hamidiye* or succumbed to the blaze.

The total casualties in Harput throughout the killings of 1894 to 1896—a spate of awful violence that became known as the Hamidian massacres—numbered about 40,000. And Harput was not the only region of the empire to suffer. All across the Ottoman Empire, Armenians were killed in cold blood. Eyewitnesses described piles of corpses, looted for their clothing and horribly mutilated postmortem, killed without regard for age or gender. They were shot, burned, drowned, and thrown into mass graves. Families were robbed of their breadwinners and starved slowly as their neighbors walked in peace thanks to a difference in race and religion. On one terrible night, 3,000 Armenians perished when the cathedral they were hiding in was burned to the ground.

The handful of Armenian revolutionaries attempted to fight back, but their efforts were to no avail. In fact, Abdul Hamid only brought an end to the violence when all of the revolutionaries had been driven out of the empire or killed. Despite pleas for international aid, no white knight would come riding to the aid of the Armenians. Even the missionaries, who came from Great Britain, America, and other countries, could do little other than to assist the survivors of the violence, people who had been left without homes, food, or families. The killing only stopped because Abdul Hamid had decided that the answer to the Armenian question had been written on the pages of history with the blood of the people.

The Hamidian massacres ended in 1896, with a death toll estimated to be as high as 300,000 people—more than one-quarter of the Armenian population of the Ottoman Empire at the time. When the violence was over, the Armenian people were left decimated, not only by the killings but also by the fact that the *Hamidiye* had forced hundreds of villages to convert to Islam or die. And while many Armenians did convert in the face of death, others refused to recant their faith. Even after the massacres, the Armenian populace in general still stubbornly held on to the Christian religion that had given them their cultural identity.

In 1905, almost ten years after the end of the massacres, Armenian revolutionaries had regrouped and attempted to assassinate Abdul Hamid, the man behind hundreds of thousands of deaths. They rigged a car with explosives and timed it to explode at the moment when Abdul Hamid normally left his favorite mosque after Friday prayers. But the attempt was ill-fated. Abdul Hamid happened to come across a friend in the mosque and spent some time talking with him, failing to come out at his usual time. The car did explode, and it took the lives of 26 people with it. But Abdul Hamid was not one of those people.

Nonetheless, his rule would not last much longer. Military coups and an unconstitutional government peppered the last few years of his reign. The time of the sultans was coming to an end. A revolution was coming—this time, though, not from bitter Armenians but from the Turkish people themselves.

Chapter 4 – The Young Turk Revolution

> "For yourselves know perfectly that the day of the Lord so cometh as a thief in the night. For when they shall say, Peace and safety; then sudden destruction cometh upon them, as travail upon a woman with child; and they shall not escape."

So wrote the apostle Paul, almost 2,000 years before the Young Turk Revolution, in a letter addressed to the budding Christian church in a city then known as Thessalonica. Then a part of Greece, Thessalonica was captured by the Ottoman Empire in the 15th century and had since become known as Salonika—and also as one of the most tolerant and culturally diverse cities in Europe.

It was ironic that Salonika was part of the Ottoman Empire, considering that the empire was one of the worst places in the world to be a religious or ethnic minority. Yet it was a strange little oasis of freedom and tolerance in the great desert of hatred that the empire had become under the reign of Abdul Hamid. In its streets, Jews and Turks, Muslims and Albanians, Armenians and Arabs were able to rub shoulders without fear of as much persecution as their fellows were suffering in the rest of the empire. And it was in Salonika that a revolution would be born—one that began with pure and just ideals but ended in genocide.

* * * *

The Young Turk Revolution occurred in 1908 in the Ottoman Empire, but its roots went as far back as Paris, 1799. The French Revolution was one of the greatest influences on the revolution that the Young Turks were planning, and many of the revolutionary leaders themselves planned their moves while they were in exile in Paris and other Western European cities.

Ever since 1878, Abdul Hamid had been ruling over the Ottoman Empire without a constitution, having suspended Parliament. His reasons for suspending the Turkish constitution were far-fetched; he claimed that democracy was not going to work until the masses had been educated, and the constitution would be reinstated once the majority of the Ottoman populace was more educated. Of course, Abdul Hamid made no attempts whatsoever to further education in his empire, and for thirty years, he simply did whatever he wanted, unbound by any constitutional laws. He was, by definition, an autocratic tyrant, and his massacre of the Armenians had made him even less popular with many of his citizens as well as the rest of Europe, who had dubbed him "the Red Sultan" for his bloody actions.

His unconstitutional government had long been chafing at his subjects, and not just with the Armenians. Powerful Turks within his administration were also looking for something different, and prominent among these were the Young Turks, a group of forward-thinking military officers. Together with several other groups that wished to promote progress in the empire, the Young Turks formed the Community of Union and Progress (CUP), a political party bent on revolution to topple the absolute monarchy once and for all.

Several smaller parties had come together to form the CUP, and one of them was the Armenian Revolutionary Federation (ARF), led by Khachatur Maloumian. The ARF had been responsible for many of the rebel activities around the same time as the Hamidian massacres, and it would have been understandable if Maloumian had viewed the Young Turks with suspicion. But at the Second Congress of the Ottoman Opposition, which was held in 1907 in Paris, the Young Turks spoke of something intoxicating and glorious, something that all Armenians desperately needed: justice. The Young Turks' vision was one of liberty, equality, justice, and freedom, one where every citizen of the empire—regardless of race or religion—would be allowed to stand on equal footing with his peers. If the Young Turks succeeded, there would be no more excessive taxation of Christian groups like the Armenians. There would be no more discrimination, oppression, or massacres. Backed by Armenian supporters, Maloumian allied his party with the CUP, and together with the Young Turks, they began to plan a revolution.

Basing many of their operations in Salonika, the Young Turks started to plan a way to bring back the constitution and get Parliament back into session. The army would be crucial to their plans. Paranoid as he was, Abdul Hamid had known for years that some of his military officers were discontent with him, so he responded by cutting the army's funding significantly, leaving the empire defenseless as other power-hungry European countries started to prey on its borders, including France, Russia, Great Britain, and Austria-Hungary. This fueled even more discontent among the military officers for whom the defense of the empire was a matter of professional pride. Once the finest military in Europe, the Ottoman Empire's army had become a joke, and its officers were not amused.

It was two of its adjutant-majors, Ismail Enver Pasha and Ahmed Niyazi—Enver Pasha was Turkish, Niyazi was Albanian—who sparked the revolt. Niyazi was the first to act on July 3rd, 1908. Abdul Hamid suspected that his loyalties did not lie with the sultan and had him investigated, and Niyazi responded by raiding the military base he commanded and then fleeing into the mountains with 200 of his followers. Enver Pasha was quick to follow, and so were many other military officers. They regrouped and then started to move on Constantinople. When Abdul Hamid tried to get the remainder of his army to go out and fight them, they refused. The sultan realized, suddenly and terribly, how defenseless he really was if his own army would not fight for him.

Three days after Niyazi's raid, the CUP issued a revolutionary proclamation. They wanted the constitution and Parliament back, and if Abdul Hamid did not comply, there would be war. Beaten, the sultan had no choice. On July 24th, he brought back Parliament, and the absolute monarchy of the Ottoman Empire was at an end.

It was a day of absolute rejoicing for the minorities of the Ottoman Empire. The celebrations turned into a loud and colorful party in the streets of Constantinople as citizens of the empire celebrated by wearing red and white, the colors of the empire's flag. Albanian and Armenian, Jewish and Greek, Turk and Arab—they all took to the streets as equals, and for one glorious day, they were united under the common title of being human.

If they had known what was coming, they would not have danced. They would have hidden.

* * * *

Adana burned and not only with fire.

Smoke towered above the city, black and thick and choking, as the scarlet flames licked around the homes of innocent families and reduced them to ashes. The streets were filled with screams, and they echoed the appearance of the fire, as blazing hatred and choking terror roared from one city block to the other. Shouts of rage, screams of pain, running feet, total anarchy—the once-prosperous city was reduced to a battleground, and the fight was cruelly unbalanced.

Elizabeth S. Webb was in the very same shoes in which Susan Wheeler had walked a path of terror and blood fourteen years earlier. Like Susan, she was an American Protestant missionary who had come to Adana to help the Christians, although their situation up until a few months ago had not been anywhere near as desperate as the predicament of the Armenians in Harput had been in Susan's time. Elizabeth had thought that she'd come to help the Armenians build better lives in a better time. Now, with horror, she was forced to witness the selfsame violence that Susan had endured in Harput.

Elizabeth was one of the foreign eyewitnesses who wrote vivid testimonies about the terrible violence that occurred in Adana in April of 1909. While the Armenians suffered far more than the American missionaries, they were not free to go home to a country that would hear them and publish detailed accounts of what had truly happened. And so, we turn to the words of these missionaries to paint a picture of the devastation that took place in Adana.

It had all started with a counter-coup. After the Young Turks succeeded in reinstating Parliament (the CUP even managed to get some seats in it), religious minorities in the country had been overjoyed to hear that they planned to abandon Abdul Hamid's policies of governing strictly in line with Islam. In fact, the CUP would stay out of religion entirely; it wished to build a secular government and allow its subjects to worship however they wanted. This caused a massive public outcry, especially from the Muslim community. When Christians were authorized to bear arms for the first time in centuries, panic began to spread. It was less than twenty years after the Hamidian massacres, after all. Would the Armenians take their revenge? Bitter and resentful, many Armenian and other Christian preachers made matters worse, pouring fuel on the fire by encouraging their members to arm themselves. A small and angry handful even abandoned the doctrine of their own churches and started to encourage the Armenians to take revenge.

Petrified, Abdul Hamid's loyalists gathered support from frightened Muslims and launched a counter-coup on April 13th, 1909. The coup was successful; the Young Turks were ousted, and for ten days of terror, Abdul Hamid reigned once more with absolute power. His message was clear. The Christians were a threat, and the Armenians needed to be exterminated.

Empowered by their taste of freedom, the Armenians refused to take this lying down. When news of the coup reached the city of Adana on April 14th, they started an angry and violent riot. The Muslim population was scared to death, believing that the Armenians were finally coming to take revenge. But the riot was nothing more than a disorganized and angry expression of a nation's fear and frustration. There was no leader of the riot, no unifying Armenian commander who could amass his people into a real threat to the Muslims. Fear and hatred, however, knows no reason. The Muslim population rose up, formed a furious mob, and fell upon the Armenians without mercy.

The violence that blossomed through Adana and its surroundings claimed almost 2,000 Turkish lives, according to the official Ottoman figures. Those same figures claim that about 5,000 Armenians were killed and that there was no massacre, simply a battle as the Turks attempted to defend themselves from marauding Armenians. Foreign witnesses, however, tell a very different story. Armenians began to flee to British and French embassies as the massacres raged on, desperate for help, and this time, Europe would not stand by and watch the slaughter. Warships were sent to pacify the situation, and courageous consulates headed out onto the streets themselves in a bid to prevent the Hamidian massacres from happening all over again.

They were only partially successful. By the end of April, the Young Turks had managed to wrest back the government and formally deposed Abdul Hamid. But the Red Sultan's swansong had cost the lives of between 20,000 and 30,000 Armenians.

Elizabeth S. Webb's account remains one of the most terrifying and vivid. She tells of how one of her American companions, clutching the hand of an Armenian preacher, tried to flee across an empty street to the safety of a mission building. The two men were in the middle of the street when an angry mob came charging toward them, armed with knives and guns. Knowing what was coming, the American seized his Armenian friend and pulled him into his arms, trying to shield him with his body. He screamed at the injustice of it, screamed that the Armenian was unarmed and harmless. There was no way that he could have hurt them, even if he wanted to. But despite the American's best efforts, the mob would have none of it. They killed him where he stood and went on with their rampage as the heartbroken American dragged his friend's dead body to safety.

To this very day, the government of Turkey denies that the Adana massacre ever happened, despite the fact that due to the many casualties three orphanages had to be built in Adana and its surroundings just to accommodate the children who had lost their parents in the violence. The Grand Vizier, Hüseyin Hilmi Pasha, went so far as to say with utter confidence that "there will never be another massacre."

He could not have been more wrong. The Hamidian and Adana massacres were just a taste of the appalling events that were to come.

Chapter 5 – The World Goes to War

The Young Turks had managed to claw back the power they had briefly lost during the counter-coup of 1909, leading many Armenians and other religious minorities to breathe a sigh of relief. Perhaps Abdul Hamid's brief and terrible return to power had been nothing more than the death throes of the old days. After all, the Young Turks had said that they would make things better.

The Young Turks did not make things better. In fact, they made them worse. The CUP deposed Abdul Hamid and put his brother, Sultan Mehmed V, on the throne; however, it was obvious that Mehmed was little more than a figurehead. The real power lay in the hands of the CUP, and it was immediately faced with a difficult new question: whether it was more important to achieve its vision of an ethnically diverse multi-national state or to keep the borders of the Ottoman Empire from further disintegrating. Every prominent power in Europe was looking for a piece of the empire, and its leaders felt besieged on every side.

Faced with the threat of invasion and of losing what remained of the Ottoman Empire, the new government began to descend into corruption. The CUP turned out not to be the savior that Turkey's people sought, and things came to a head when the new government was forced to decide what would be its greatest priority: promoting the peaceful coexistence of a diverse and varied people within the empire or avoiding the loss of imperial lands to the rest of the world. History might have turned out very differently if the CUP had chosen to emphasize the former at the cost of losing some of its lands and power. Instead, it was decided that it would be more important to present a united front and avoid the further loss of lands to the predatory powers of the rest of Europe, and so, the CUP attempted to unite the Ottoman Empire under one singular identity: that of being Turkish.

It might have worked if everyone in the Ottoman Empire really was Turkish. But they weren't; while Turks made up the majority of the population, there were also Armenians, Arabs, Albanians, Jews, Greeks, other minorities who did not identify as being Turkish. They spoke a different language, worshiped a different god, and had an entirely separate culture and identity. For the Armenians, who had clung so stubbornly to their ways even in the face of massacres and who had been hoping so desperately for change under the Young Turk regime, it was a terrible blow to be told that they now had to be Turkish.

Turkification, as the CUP's new policy became known, was an old idea, dating back to the end of the 19th century as part of the Ottoman Empire's bid for unification. It was the Young Turks, however, who really brought Turkification into full force in the 1910s. Turkification was an attempt to wholly assimilate the minorities within the empire, transforming all of the peoples into Turks.

The leaders of the CUP at the time, who were the real rulers of the Ottoman Empire as the sultans had been reduced to little more than figureheads, were a triumvirate of powerful officials in the government. Mehmed Talaat Pasha was the Grand Vizier; Ismail Enver Pasha, who had been one of the first military commanders involved in the Young Turk Revolution, was the Minister of War;

and Ahmed Djemal Pasha was the Minister of the Navy. They would go down in history as the "Three Pashas," and all three of them firmly believed that Turkification would lead to power and unity for the Ottoman Empire and thus security for its people as well as power for themselves. If thousands of people had to give up their way of living and their faith, then it would be a necessary sacrifice to secure their safety.

They could not have been more wrong. Instead of uniting the citizens of the empire under one uniform culture, Turkification created tremendous rifts between the Turks and the minorities who had just started on the road to reconciliation. Brainwashed by government propaganda that all non-Turks were inferior and dangerous, Turks once more found themselves viewing minorities—not just Armenians—with deep suspicion. Enraged by the fact that they had effectively been told to abandon their own culture, many Armenians responded by refusing to become Turkified at all. They also refused to convert to Islam.

While outright persecution did not begin immediately, Armenians certainly felt the pinch of Turkification very early on. They were still being taxed more harshly than their Muslim counterparts and were denied many of the privileges that their fellow citizens were enjoying by virtue of simply being Turkish. Worse, the official language used in courts and other government institutions throughout the Ottoman Empire had been changed to Turkish, which many Armenians and other minorities did not speak. The Three Pashas had tried to assimilate the minorities of the empire; instead, they had succeeded in alienating them even further.

The First Balkan War was evidence of how badly Turkification was failing to create unity. Tired of oppression and disappointed that the Young Turks had failed to deliver everything that they had promised, a group of ethnic minorities living in the Ottoman Empire appealed to their native countries for help. In response, Greece, Serbia, Bulgaria, and Montenegro—all newly independent from the empire but all with ethnic populations still residing alongside the

Ottomans—joined forces against the Turks. Known as the Balkan League, these allies declared war on the Turks in 1912, and they fought a brutal and bloody war against them. The war was ugly but also short-lived; by the end of the year, the Ottoman Empire had lost most of its vast European territories to the Balkan League. Instead of reforming their policies toward minorities, however, the Three Pashas saw the First Balkan War as being symptomatic of the problem of having non-Turks within the empire. Turkification was forced harder and harder on the minorities.

As discontent spread like a disease through the empire, it would soon face much bigger problems. For the first time in history, the entire world was about to go to war.

* * * *

The Europe of 1914 was tinder, drenched in lighter fluid. All it would take was a single spark to set the whole continent—and, with it, the rest of the world—alight. And that spark would find its origins in the Second Balkan War.

After winning many territories back from the Ottoman Empire, the members of the Balkan League almost immediately started fighting among themselves over how to split the spoils of the war. The territories that the victors had gained were considerable, and it caused a profound rift between the members of the League. By 1913, Greece and Serbia had formed an alliance against Bulgaria. In retaliation, Bulgaria turned to its powerful neighbor, Austria, for help. Austria was not an inconsiderable power at the time, and Greece and Serbia saw this as a significant threat. They declared war on Bulgaria in the summer of 1913.

The Second Balkan War, like its predecessor, was as savage as it was short-lived. In only two months, Bulgaria—despite its mighty ally—had been brought to its knees. Greece and Serbia got what they wanted, but it was still clear that Bulgaria and Austria together were a threat to the countries that were just starting to recover from centuries of Ottoman rule.

The rest of Europe was similarly embroiled in simmering conflicts. Complicated alliances patterned Europe and Asia: Serbia was in alliance with Russia, which was allied with France, which was an ally of Great Britain, which in turn was allied with Japan. Any move from a single country could trigger a snowball effect of wars with other countries as they moved to defend their allies. The Ottoman Empire, for its part, was not officially allied with anyone in this way but retained its good relationship with Germany, knowing that trouble was coming.

Tensions over imperial lands in Africa and Asia contributed to an arms race between the countries as each tried to prove to the other that it was too powerful to attack. As a result, by 1914, the whole of Europe was armed to the teeth and spoiling for a fight. All it needed was a reason, and a Serbian man named Gavrilo Princip would provide the reason for a war that would claim almost seventeen million lives.

Princip was a Serbian nationalist. While Serbia had fought against Austria in the Second Balkan War, there were still Serbs and other Slavic peoples living in Austria at the time, and they desired freedom from Austria's imperialistic ideals, which dated back to its glory days as the seat of the Habsburg rulers of the Holy Roman Empire centuries before. It was a Serbian terrorist group, known as the Black Hand, that would eventually decide to do something less than diplomatic about this problem. And Princip was the trigger finger of the Black Hand—a fact that he proved when he assassinated Austrian heir apparent Archduke Franz Ferdinand and his wife, Sophie, on June 28th, 1914.

At once, the whole of Europe was in a total uproar. Austria was determined to open war on Serbia, but it was forced to hesitate because of Serbia's powerful ally Russia, which had even more powerful allies of its own. Austria, however, was backed by the German Kaiser Wilhelm II. Bolstered by the knowledge of its own strong ally, Austria-Hungary gave Serbia an impossible ultimatum. The ultimatum, which demanded that Serbia should allow their enemies to investigate the assassination in Serbia, had been drafted with the knowledge that it could not possibly have been accepted. It was not so much a way out of the war as a way to shift the blame for it. Serbia, left without a choice, responded by declaring war. Within days, Austria-Hungary and Germany found themselves facing a conflict not only with Serbia but also with Russia and its allies, Great Britain, France, and Belgium.

August 4th, 1914, marked the beginning of the war. Germany spearheaded an invasion into France while at the same time launching an attack on Russia in the east. The effect on France was utterly devastating as brilliant German commanders devastated the country, taking the city of Liège by August 15th.

For several months, the Ottoman Empire, which was not directly involved in the conflict, sat back and watched as Europe burned. And the Three Pashas had a good reason for not wanting to get involved in what was blossoming into the First World War. Decades of war and revolution had left the Ottoman Empire depleted and exhausted, and as the fragile Young Turk movement struggled to pick up the pieces after the devastating First Balkan War, it appeared that engaging in the First World War would be disastrous. However, as Germany began to amass victory after victory, Enver Pasha started to reconsider. Joining the war on the German side could be a blessing for the Ottoman Empire if it ended in victory. It could be the Hail Mary that the empire needed to solidify its rapidly crumbling borders—a last bid to gain back its old power.

Despite opposition from the prime minister, Enver Pasha quickly gained the support of the other two Pashas, and the Ottoman Empire entered World War I on October 28th, 1914, fighting alongside Germany.

Most of the fighting in which the Ottomans became involved would occur in the Middle East and the Balkans, not directly within the empire's borders. Dismayed, its citizens would still be forced to witness, after having endured massacres and a revolution, a new evil: a world war. What could possibly be worse?

They would soon find out the answer to that question.

Chapter 6 – Red Sunday

Soghomon Soghomonian had probably first heard the words of "Dle Yaman" on the flanks of Mount Ararat when he was a freshly orphaned preteen. Back in the 1880s, it was a love song, and the passionate edge of its lyrics blew across the mountain breeze to light something in young Soghomon's heart. The song was desperate and whimsical and lovesick.

Alas! Alas! Our homes face each other,

Oh, alas! Isn't it enough that my eyes send you a sign?

Alas! Alas! Oh my love!

Oh, alas! Isn't it enough that my eyes send you a sign?

Little did Soghomon know that "Dle Yaman" would one day be so much more than a folksy old love song, especially to him. It would become a song of loss, a loss so deep and palpable that the whole world felt the brunt of its agony.

* * * *

Soghomon Soghomonian, born a Christian Armenian in 1869, is better known by his ordained name of Komitas. Not only was he a leader in the Armenian Church, but he also grew up to become a singer and composer who would single-handedly build the foundation for Armenian folk music as it is known today. And like 235 fellow Armenians, Komitas was deported on the day the Armenian Genocide began: April 24th, 1915.

Ever since the Ottoman Empire had joined World War I, life had gotten progressively harder for the Armenians, particularly because the Islamic religious authorities took the opportunity to declare war too. Their war, however, would not be against the enemies of Germany. It would be a holy war, a jihad against all non-Christians (except for their allies in World War I, conveniently). This meant that even the Armenian citizens within the Ottoman Empire itself would not be spared. The hope that the revolution of 1908 had brought was now soundly snuffed out as another wave of oppression crushed the Armenians. Muslims viewed them as a target, and even secular leaders viewed them with suspicion and even fear. Since the Ottomans had spent decades making life unbearable for all Armenian people, it would be no surprise if the Armenians decided to betray the Ottoman Empire in favor of neighboring Russia. To this end, the government launched a campaign to remove all weapons from Armenian possession. The people were stripped of anything that could be used for either revolt or self-defense, down to their very kitchen knives.

Some of the Armenians certainly were ready to ally with Russia, hoping that their lives would be a little better in a Christian country. The majority, however, simply attempted to continue with their daily lives as well as they could in the face of a world war. They were just ordinary people doing ordinary things. They posed little threat, but Enver Pasha would not be persuaded to believe this.

This became evident when Enver Pasha took his army to Sarikamish, Russia. He planned to claim back some of the lands that the Ottomans had lost to Russia in the Russo-Turkish War in the 1870s, but it was an ambitious plan doomed to fail, and Enver Pasha's army was all but destroyed by Russian troops. Enraged, Enver Pasha blamed the Armenians in the area, saying that they had sided with the Russians and caused the loss of countless Turkish lives. This was not entirely untrue; it was accurate that some Armenian volunteers had joined the Russian tsar's forces, but their numbers and forces were not to blame for the defeat. Instead, it was more likely due to Enver Pasha's incompetence.

Nonetheless, panic about perceived dangers from Armenians, fueled by propaganda, spread throughout the Ottoman army, and the Armenian men who had been drafted into the army were removed from passive duty, stripped of their arms, and transferred to so-called labor battalions to do the boring, laborious work of warfare. Thus, Enver Pasha attempted to ensure that every Armenian in the empire was disarmed.

By April 1915, tensions were skyrocketing throughout the Ottoman Empire. While some Armenians had joined forces with the Russians, the vast majority of them were terrified and helpless within the empire—and for good reason. Violent gangs of criminals began to form with one intent: to kill the Armenians. And the Turkish police did little to stop them as chaos blossomed across the empire, with Armenians being driven out of their homes and butchered in the streets by the gangs.

The violence was particularly harsh in the area of Van, an Ottoman city near the Russian border. Armenians in the towns and villages surrounding Van found themselves at war with the gangs that sought to murder them all; the police were no help whatsoever, and the Armenians had been deprived of any means to defend themselves from their marauding enemies. Desperate, thousands of Armenians fled to the city itself. Despite being grossly outnumbered by the Turks, the Armenians engaged in a bloody and disorganized hand-to-hand battle in the streets of Van. Thousands perished, but eventually, they managed to gain control over the city. Keeping the gates open for refugees, who streamed in from the surrounding countryside in vast numbers, the Armenians prayed that Van would prove to be a safe refuge. Yet with only 1,500 men to defend it (armed with about 1,000 pistols and 300 rifles, which was fewer guns than men), the situation remained appallingly grim.

It would soon become grimmer still. On April 19th, 1915, a military commander named Jevdet Bey commanded the city to surrender 4,000 conscripts for the labor battalions. His command was a poor pretense; the Armenians were well aware that if they sent him those men, they would be promptly executed. Trying to buy some time, they offered to send him 500 men and some exemption money instead. But Jevdet refused. He never wanted soldiers; he wanted blood, and he would get it. Calling the Armenians rebellious (which they certainly were, but they were facing mass persecution), Jevdet angrily claimed that he was going to kill "every Christian man, woman and child" in the city.

If peaceful surrender had been an option, it is possible the Armenians might have taken it. The odds were terrible; Jevdet had at his command about 5,000 seasoned soldiers, and Enver Pasha's 1st Expeditionary Force—numbering around 60,000—was nearby. The Armenians must have known that to fight back would mean they would die, but at least they would die fighting instead of being brutally executed in cold blood.

Things came to a head on April 20th, 1915. A lone woman—bruised, battered, exhausted, and traumatized beyond all expression—came stumbling across the ravaged countryside, heading for the oasis of peace that she hoped Van would be. She had survived so much, and she was utterly desperate, desperate enough that in her panicking flight toward the city, she strayed too close to the Ottoman soldiers. They seized her, and their intentions were clear as they pawed at her body and pushed her around. Unable to watch, a pair of Armenian men burst out of Van and rushed to her aid. Their effort was as pathetic as it was courageous. They were promptly shot, one after the other, and Jevdet saw this as the perfect excuse to attack. He sent his soldiers forward, and the siege of Van, which is often referred to as the Defense of Van, began.

Hopelessly outnumbered though they were, the Armenians succeeded in keeping the city gates open to the rivers of refugees that continued to pour into the city; at this point, there were about

45,000 vulnerable innocents inside the city, defended by a mere courageous handful. Despite the best efforts of their shoestring guard, thousands of the refugees were butchered.

Still, the Ottoman government had not yet actually made it legal to kill Armenians. But all that would change on April 24th, 1915. The Defense of Van was still raging when, 785 miles away, an official act of ruthless persecution against ethnic Armenians would take place in the very capital of the Ottoman Empire.

Constantinople was not the jewel of culture and commerce that it had been in the era of the Byzantine Empire, but it was nonetheless a center of academia and art in the Ottoman Empire. Despite the disadvantages imposed upon them by their race, many Armenians had managed to make names for themselves as important intellectuals within the city. Soghomon Soghomonian, by this time known as Father Komitas, was one of them. Having spent years traveling the world and performing Armenian folk music, Komitas had become something of a celebrity. It would perhaps have been wiser for him to stay in Europe, where most people were sympathetic to the Armenian cause and saw him as a tragic but wonderful artist; instead, he had come home to Constantinople.

Like hundreds of other Armenian intellectuals, Komitas was peacefully passing the evening of April 23rd, 1915, when the Ottomans came. Storming into homes and workplaces, Turkish soldiers and police arrested a total of about 235 Armenian intellectuals that night. They no longer had the right to be citizens of the Ottoman Empire, they were told. They would be briefly held in cells in Constantinople before being deported to the Syrian Desert.

Over the next few days, thousands more Armenians were rounded up and forced out of the city. In the meantime, Van continued to stand against Jevdet's angry horde; in fact, the siege would continue until May 17th when Russian relief forces would finally come to the rescue. It was still too late for about 50,000 Armenians, some of them soldiers but many of them petrified refugees that had fled to the city. Those who survived maintained control of the city with the help of the Russians.

By that time, thousands more Armenians were being forced to leave the empire that had been so cruel to them yet was the only home their people had known for thousands of years. While many of the intellectuals arrested on April 24th were executed, Komitas survived, but only as a shadow of his former self. The events of the deportation—and, along the way, the rape and execution of hundreds of Armenians—would leave a scar on his mind that never could heal.

Nobody could blame him, for what Komitas and others had to endure was nothing short of a death march.

Chapter 7 – Death March

Illustration II: Refugees in a Syrian camp

Considering that Armin T. Wegner was a member of the German army, it was a little surprising that he chose to become one of the Armenians' greatest allies.

When war broke out in 1914, Wegner—then 28 years old—could not face the idea of taking up arms expressly to kill others. He had to join the army, however, and he did so as a combat medic. Always driven by a strongly altruistic desire to make the world a better place, Wegner had little taste for war itself, but he certainly had no lack of courage. Shortly after being sent to the Middle Eastern front, he earned an Iron Cross for his bravery in helping wounded soldiers under heavy fire.

But Wegner hadn't just come to help the wounded. He'd come to document the events of the war—and he had long been suspicious that the Ottoman Empire's policy against Armenians was not the act of defense that its leadership claimed. The leaders of the Ottoman Empire had protested that deporting all of the Armenians was its only choice in order to protect itself from rebellious alliances between Armenians and Russians. Wegner had a hunch that this wasn't true. But what he would witness was far worse than anything he could have ever imagined.

The arrest of several thousand Armenians in Constantinople in April 1915 was only the beginning of the deportations. The Ottoman government wanted them gone, and they would march those Armenians across the brutal Syrian Desert in the growing heat of summer and then dump them in the small town of Deir ez-Zor in Syria. The town could not possibly accommodate the masses of Armenians that were flooding in, but the Ottomans were not concerned with this. All of the Armenians could perish in that desert for all they cared.

And those masses of Armenians were truly massive. When Talaat and the other two Pashas first ordered the deportation of Armenians, it was supposed to include only those who had been involved in the violence in Van and other areas of the Ottoman Empire (violence which, ironically, Talaat referred to as "massacres"). By May 29th, 1915, a new law had been passed. This Tehcir Law was the death knell for hundreds of thousands of Armenian people.

The Tehcir Law allowed Ottoman officials to summarily deport, without any form of trial or investigation and at their discretion, any Armenian person that was viewed to be a threat to national security.

Of course, for many officials, there was no need to sense a threat at all. Simply being Armenian was reason enough for thousands of innocent people to be arrested, and once they were arrested, they were sent to the Syrian Desert to die.

Many did not even make it that far. The forced removal of the Armenians from the Ottoman Empire was utterly brutal. Coming from the cool green mountainsides of Anatolia, the Armenians were forced to make their way, generally on foot, across the stark landscape of the desert.

All of them suffered; relief was offered only in a tiny degree to the very rich, who were able to pay off guards to give them more food. But one has to let one's heart wander to those who were only children when the genocide began. To follow the journey of an Armenian child along one of those death marches is almost incomprehensible; the suffering that all of those people endured (or failed to endure) is almost too hard to imagine. But for the sake of the fallen, let us attempt to imagine it. Let us attempt to imagine what it would be like to be an Armenian child dragged from a rural home in the green foothills where your ancestors had lived long before the Ottoman Empire even had a name.

Roughly arrested by police, military, or ordinary Turkish citizens (who were, in many cases, given free rein to "assist" the military in the arrest and persecution of Armenians), you and your family would possibly be held in some dank and overcrowded cell for a brief time while other people like you were rounded up. Did the children ask questions? Did they want their parents to tell them why these scary men were dragging them away? Did they ask what they'd done wrong? Did they see their own mothers and fathers cry? Or was it worse than that—were they stripped away from their families and carried off by brutal strangers into the night?

If you were a woman or even a comely enough young girl, your lot was even unhappier than that of your male counterparts. Fueled by uncontrolled rage and desire, having left their own wives or girlfriends behind to join the army, the soldiers were savage in their treatment of the women and girls. Mothers were raped in front of their children, brides in front of their grooms. Sometimes repeatedly, their bodies were violated over and over by multiple men until they were left to die by the wayside or perhaps stripped naked and sold into slavery in one of the cities.

Stripped of dignity, stripped of the innocence of childhood, stripped perhaps of your mother or sisters or your own rights to your body, you would then be forced to begin the march. Perhaps by this time, your father or brother had tried to stand up to the soldiers and had been beaten to death or run through with a sword. Perhaps your family was still clinging to each other as you were herded like abused cattle toward the Syrian Desert. Some lucky few—how lucky they were is debatable—were driven like livestock onto the cattle cars on trains. Crammed together with only standing room, they were forced to endure the long journey by rail without food or water or even somewhere to go to the bathroom. The reek of excrement must have filled those cars until the air was almost impossible to breathe. In those windowless cars, motion sickness must have been inevitable, and there was nowhere to vomit except on the people surrounding you. Sickness spread in those cars like wildfire.

Those who were not loaded onto the cars had no choice but to walk. And the distance of that walk can hardly be thought of in terms of something that any human being is capable of. The Armenians arrested in Constantinople would be forced to walk almost one thousand miles to Deir ez-Zor. Whether they were old or young, sickly or strong, whether they had small children or grandmothers with them, or whether they were pregnant, ill, lame, or disabled, the Armenians had to move—and they had to move at a pace dictated by (comparatively) well-fed soldiers who were mostly fit young men. To fail to keep up was to be butchered brutally and with a sword. The killings by sword were done expressly to traumatize the witnesses. If you were a child, you might have to watch your parents or your siblings or your old grandparent die in a gruesome manner.

If you were a child, you were unlikely to have survived this far. The provisions that the Turkish government had made for those stumbling across the desert were utterly pitiful; in fact, the lack of provisions for food, water, or shelter that was made would later be part of the argument that what the Ottoman Empire had done was truly genocide instead of war. When the government sent those Armenians off into the desert, it was with the full knowledge that most of them would not survive. The aim was not to deport a group of rebels. The aim was to annihilate an entire cultural group.

Perhaps even worse than the starvation—which was so severe that the Armenians found themselves picking through crops for raw grains just to get something into their stomachs—was the heat. Most of the hapless victims were used to the cool, crisp air of the mountains. Now, they found themselves moving through the utter dryness of the desert without free access to potable water. They became dehydrated and died along the way in the thousands, with no shelter from the shade as they were forced to march in the heat of the day. If you were a child, clutching your mother's hand (if your mother, despite the raping and the abuse, had survived), you would see mounds of corpses lying along the roadside as you walked. Some of them would be decomposed or torn by scavenging animals. Flies would walk across their glassy eyes as they stared up at the pitiless sky, and you, a mere child, would see more death in a day than most ever see in a lifetime. Some of the corpses were buried in mass graves (60,000 Armenians were discovered in one grave alone in 1916), while others were simply left in the sun to rot.

To make matters even worse, if you were a child, you would witness the total disintegration of the mental state of many of the adults around you. Perhaps even adults that you looked up to, adults that you trusted. The psychological effects of witnessing and surviving the terror and destruction that was being wrought on their people were profound for many of the Armenians. Komitas was one of them. The mind that could pull a melody out of thin air, the heart that beat so passionately for the Armenian people, the soul that had been so wholly committed to his faith, was now reduced to a petrified shadow of itself. Komitas spent much of his time clinging to anyone he knew, babbling senselessly, every rock and boulder imagined to be a guard aiming a gun at him. He would not be the only one.

And hundreds of soldiers were either partaking in this violence and brutality or were a silent witness to it. Some of them must have felt a sense of injustice. As the bodies of innocents began to heap up by the roadside, surely there must have been some awareness that humanity had just crossed the line from warfare into something even darker. This was more than destroying a threat to national security. This was the destruction of an entire race. Yet many of them either continued to rape and kill wantonly or simply kept their mouths shut and their eyes blind to the appalling scene before them.

Armin T. Wegner, however, was not one of them. He had brought his camera to the front lines, and despite considerable threats from his superiors and the Ottomans, he used it. Smuggling the plates back home so that nobody could find them, Wegner documented the atrocities before him, despite the fact that they were being committed by his country's allies. His photographs continue the gruesome story of the death marches, images almost too heart-wrenching and too appalling to look at. A desperate and bewildered Armenian priest, overwhelmed by the number of dead for whom he wished to perform funeral rites. The skeletal corpses of children who starved to death, their bodies nothing more than bones with a thin covering of skin, their lips even drawn back from their teeth with the sparsity of their bodies. The hollow eyes of the orphans, staring blankly into the camera, the horror behind their eyes almost too much to begin to imagine. Disease sweeping through their pathetic camps and leaving behind piles of corpses.

Hundreds of thousands of Armenians died in the most horrible ways on those awful death marches. So much so that only 45,000 actually made it to Deir ez-Zor. And once they reached their destination, it would not be the end of their suffering. But Wegner was not the only voice speaking out against the destruction of the Armenian people. Thanks to the telegram, the rest of the world was listening as well.

Chapter 8 – One Thousand Orphans

Wegner was not the only one who would raise his voice against what was happening in the Ottoman Empire. In fact, just like the missionaries who worked in the Hamidian and Adana massacres, many Americans would also speak out against the madness, sparking a wave of support in the United States as it entered WWI on the Allied side.

The American ambassador to the Ottoman Empire told his superiors how the Three Pashas had given "the death warrant to a whole race," and how even in their conversations with him, officials made no attempt to pretend that the deportation of the Armenians was anything other than a bid to exterminate them. There was no word for "genocide" in 1915, but Ambassador Henry Morgenthau's description was almost more vivid: he called it "race murder." The invention of the telegram had made it possible to transmit information across the world far more quickly than a letter, and it wasn't long before news of the genocide reached U.S. shores. The *New York Times* had already run a story about an impending massacre early in 1915, and now, it kept citizens informed of atrocity after atrocity being committed in the Ottoman Empire. Considering that the U.S. and the Ottomans were enemies during the war, it is certainly possible that some propaganda was involved. But when concerned Americans started to make an effort to help, it became clear that the story of the Armenians' fate was more than just a nightmare. It was very, very real.

The American Committee for Armenian and Syrian Relief (ACASR) was formed and was strongly supported by President Woodrow Wilson. During the genocide and especially in the years to follow, donations and volunteers flooded into the Ottoman Empire to try to help the beleaguered Armenians and other minority groups that were also being persecuted. Tragically, despite their best efforts, these volunteers were not able to do much. The Ottomans—perhaps a little surprised that some Armenians had actually made it to Deir ez-Zor— were not done yet. They would not rest until the Armenian population had been decimated.

* * * *

Ali Suad Bey could not believe his eyes.

The governor of the area around Deir ez-Zor, Ali Bey, was well versed in warfare. He was, after all, a military commander; he had seen his fair share of trouble. But nothing like this.

Ali Bey watched in utter horror as tens of thousands of Armenians came stumbling into his domain from the desert. They had just walked hundreds of miles across the Syrian Desert in midsummer, and they were all exhausted, sick, and dehydrated. Most of them were women and children; the majority of the men had been systematically killed en route. In fact, the overwhelming majority were orphaned children. They had dark, hollow eyes that seemed blank and empty thanks to the atrocities that they had witnessed, set in skeletal faces, their cheeks pinched and pale, scarred by the brutal sun. Their chapped lips were stretched thin over teeth that protruded with emaciation. All they could think about was survival. They were utterly desperate for food and water, their hair crawling with lice and wounds covering their unwashed little bodies. Ali Bey could not grasp why his government considered them such a terrible threat to national security. They were only children—traumatized, terrified, orphaned children who had endured more in the past summer than most people would ever have to see in an entire lifetime.

Ali Bey was also somewhat surprised to see them. The Turkish government had not been concerned in the slightest about what they would actually do with the Armenians once they had reached the end of the deportation; in fact, they seemed mildly surprised that any of them had survived the death marches at all. No provision whatsoever had been made to receive the deportees once they had reached Deir ez-Zor. Ali Bey was appalled and also determined to make an attempt to accommodate the 30,000 starving Armenians that were trickling onto his doorstep. There was luckily a large cave nearby that could serve as a temporary shelter from the sweltering August sun, but it could by no means accommodate that many people. Ali Bey had a real problem on his hands, and the rest of the Ottoman administration had no interest whatsoever in helping him.

Nonetheless, this courageous Arab was not about to give up on the thousands of helpless people who were now dependent on him. He strove to build refugee camps as well as he could, and for a brief time, the Armenians were provided with the rights that they had been so sorely deprived of during the death marches. Ali Bey provided them with food, water, shelter, and even medical care and protection to the best of his abilities. It could not have been easy; government funding must have been practically nonexistent for this project, and Ali Bey was almost completely alone in his efforts. To this end, he personally took in about one thousand orphans, feeding them probably out of his own pocket or possibly even plundering the coffers of the city to provide for its influx of refugees. He was determined that the Armenian Genocide—which had already claimed hundreds of thousands, if not over a million, lives on the death marches—would end with him.

If only he had been left alone to do what he was doing, Ali Bey might have succeeded, too. But it was not to be.

The Armenians, by this point, had been thrown out of the Ottoman Empire. Those who were sheltering under Ali Bey's wings were largely women and children. None of them were soldiers, and it's unlikely that any of them had shown even a smattering of rebellion. To survive the death march was to be wholly submissive; to show any spark of resistance was to die brutally in front of your watching family. Those refugees were survivors, but they were also as beaten as a human being can be. They had lost everything—their homes, businesses, jobs, families. It is inconceivable that 30,000 half-starved Armenians could be any form of a threat to the Ottoman Empire, which mobilized nearly three million soldiers during the extent of the First World War. Yet Talaat Pasha, Minister of the Interior, was not concerned with the Armenians being a threat. He hated the fact that they even existed, and this was made abundantly clear in a cipher he sent to Deir ez-Zor in September 1915. Talaat forbade the court-martial of any soldier who had committed crimes against the Armenians; he also forbade the Armenians to open any lawsuits against the Ottoman military or government.

The final straw came in mid-September 1915. By this point, the Armenians had been sheltering in Deir ez-Zor for some time, and they had established a little town of their own. Trade was starting to take place among them; they were remembering their songs and stories, their skills. They were starting to live life again despite the misery of what they had experienced—after all, the Armenians were nothing if not survivors. They were starting to find their way back to a semblance of normality, thanks to the efforts of Ali Suad Bey.

Then the orders came from Ali Bey's superior, Governor-General Abdülhalik Renda. He told Ali Bey that allowing thousands of Armenians to live peacefully in their new "home" was "an instance of disagreement with the sacred goal of the government." "Expel them from that place!" he ordered vehemently.

Ali Bey was well aware, and his superior made it clear, that their "sacred goal" was to kill every Armenian on the face of the earth. Ali Bey's response was calm and simple. "The means of transportation do not exist so that I could deport the people," he told his superior. The "means of transportation" that had been used to get them to Deir ez-Zor in the first place—the Armenians' own feet—certainly existed, but Ali Bey was making it clear that he was not going to send the refugees on another death march. He made his stance abundantly clear in the second sentence of his telegram: "If the goal being pursued is to kill them, I can neither do it, nor make it done."

Nothing was going to persuade Ali Bey to hurt the people that he was protecting. And so, he was summarily removed from his position. In his place, the Ottoman government installed Zeki Bey, a military commander who had already proven himself to be exceptionally brutal and cruel in warfare. To bully other soldiers in battle was one thing; to bully 30,000 helpless Armenians was a delight in itself in the eyes of Zeki Bey, and he fell upon his duty to make the Armenians' lives as unbearable as possible with unfettered zeal.

Under Zeki Bey, the refugee camps that Ali Bey had so lovingly set up became death camps, a harrowing precursor of what the Jewish would suffer at the hands of the Nazis in the Second World War. Food and water were immediately withheld, beatings and rapes were once again commonplace, and any fragment of hope or joy that the Armenians had found in their lives was once again removed and ruthlessly destroyed. The killings began again as thousands of children starved to death and thousands of Armenians were cast out of the camps to wander the banks of the Euphrates and die in the desert.

Saddest of all, the one thousand orphans that Ali Bey had set up in a large house and cared for personally were all thrown out onto the street. Zeki Bey did not attempt to shoot or drown them. He didn't have to. He just left them on the streets to starve. And starve they did, perhaps still begging at the doors of the home where they had so briefly found joy, until they collapsed and died in the gutters, naked and alone.

Chapter 9 – The Black Sea Runs Red

Illustration III: Henry Morgenthau's image of massacred Armenian corpses. This was a common sight in the countryside of the Ottoman Empire

Eitan Belkind, Aaron Aaronsohn, and some of their associates were agronomists. At least, so the Ottoman government thought.

Eitan had been serving in the Ottoman military since he was a teenager, but he had never really been a man of war. Raised in a

Jewish home, Eitan had faced discrimination similar to that suffered by his Armenian counterparts. Jews at the time feared being conscripted into the Ottoman army, but when Eitan's time came to join the military, he managed to serve in roles that didn't involve shooting a gun. First, his fluency in four different languages earned him a post as a translator. Then, in March 1915—a month before the beginning of the Armenian Genocide and after having witnessed the brutal deportation of hundreds of his own people—Eitan was assigned to work on an infestation of locusts that was sweeping across the country. Aaron Aaronsohn was the leader of this project, and Eitan became his secretary.

Now in his twenties, he was working in the city of Trebizond (modern-day Trabzon), located on the banks of the Black Sea. As a higher-ranking official, despite being a Jew, Eitan was allowed to move around the countryside more or less as he wished. He and Aaron were out in the county near the Euphrates River going about their locust-killing business in the company of some Ottoman soldiers when they saw it. A corpse. It floated quietly along, face-down, on the waters of the Euphrates. It was stripped naked, and as it floated by, Eitan could see every bone in its body. He could count the vertebrae. He could see the water lapping in the deep hollows between its ribs.

Eitan and Aaron both expressed surprise, but the Ottoman guards nearby were not flustered. They shrugged, laughing it off, saying that it was okay because it was just an Armenian. There was a camp some way up the river, and the Ottoman guards were systematically killing the Armenians—especially the orphans—by binding their hands and feet and then hurling them into the river.

The horrified Eitan would soon witness one of the most terrible mass killings that took place during the Armenian Genocide. While many of the Armenians had already died on the marches to Deir ez-Zor and other concentration camps, and many more were currently starving quietly to death, there were quicker and more popular ways of killing them, too. Driven by brainwashing and bloodlust, Turkish soldiers got more and more inventive with their methods of murdering the Armenians by the hundreds. Merely shooting them seemed far too merciful for so dangerous and evil a people as the Armenians; instead, they took to dousing them (especially orphans) in gasoline and then setting them on fire. Drowning was also popular, and here in Trebizond, the killers were spoiled as they could choose between the Euphrates and the Black Sea.

Eitan made it his mission to find out what was happening to the Armenians, and what he saw was horrifying. His eyewitness account describes the most terrible scenes: the appalling concentration camps, where his Armenian friend, Shirinyan, found his own family starving to death; the screams of women, heard in the night, and the later discovery of beheaded children floating in the bloodstained Euphrates; Arab sheiks pawing through Armenian women to find wives (whose husbands would be slaughtered once the sheik made his choice, if they hadn't been killed already) as their people were being murdered within sight of them; the burning of five thousand Armenians tied to a pile of blazing dry grass.

But worst of all was a scene witnessed from the banks of the Black Sea itself. A scene that would see the Black Sea's waters turn crimson.

* * * *

In Eitan's wanderings among the Armenians, their awful plight must have sparked in him a dark suspicion: someone, some specific person in the government of Trebizond and its surroundings, must be behind all of this. That man was Cemal Azmi, the governor of Trebizond.

Before the genocide began in earnest, Azmi had been one of the founders of the so-called Special Organization. Officially, the Special Organization existed chiefly to reopen Parliament after it was closed by Abdul Hamid, but it continued after the reopening with one cold goal: to suppress the enemies of the Ottoman Empire. And now that the empire had deemed the Armenians its enemies, many members of the Special Organization were now among the chief perpetrators of the genocide.

Azmi was no exception. He earned his nickname "the butcher of Trebizond" by ordering many of the awful killings that Eitan had witnessed, including the burning of those five thousand people outside Trebizond. But the gruesome burnings, drownings, and shootings of innocent and unarmed people were not Azmi's only methods of disposing of the Armenians that he hated so much. He had more insidious ways—ways to get to those lucky handfuls of Armenians that had not been deported at all, ways to strike at them right where they felt safest: in the hospital for routine vaccinations or procedures.

At the time, typhus was sweeping through the war-torn empire, particularly in the concentration camps or areas impoverished by decades of massacre and war. In the modern day, typhus is treatable with antibiotics. In the winter of 1914 to 1916, decades before the discovery of penicillin, it was a death sentence even to fairly healthy people; to the starved and stressed victims of genocide, it was almost invariably fatal.

To many, the typhus epidemic was just a tragedy upon all the other tragedies that were taking place in the empire, but to Azmi, it was potentially a weapon. Normally spread by human body lice (which were utterly abundant in the concentration camps), typhus could also be spread purposefully by other means, and Azmi quickly persuaded some of the doctors at the Trebizond Red Crescent Hospital to carry out the dirty deed. Under the pretense of giving routine vaccinations, a handful of doctors at the hospital started drawing blood from patients who were sick and feverish with typhoid. Then, when Armenians who were due to be deported came into the hospital, they were given that disease-ridden blood. Artificially assisted in this way, the typhus epidemic became even more rampant. And the bacteria causing the disease was not the only thing that the doctors were giving the innocent people—particularly children—who came into the hospital. Countless children were overdosed with morphine to the point that they died. The doctors, who had been educated in order to help people, were killing them by the hundreds.

But it wasn't good enough for Azmi. Perhaps the doctors simply weren't killing enough people; perhaps the reason for Azmi's impatience was darker than that. Given his penchant for killing children, perhaps Azmi was driven by bloodlust to the extent that he wanted to see the Armenians suffer. Irritated by the hospital's methodical eradication of its Armenian patients, Azmi ordered thousands of Armenian women and children (there were very few men left alive by this point) to be rounded up and taken to the docks.

Once these innocent people had been taken to the shores, they were told that they were being deported to another town across the Black Sea. Figuring that being deported from one hellish area to another couldn't be any worse than staying in Trebizond, the people climbed on board the ships and waited as they were taken out upon the icy winter waters of the Black Sea. But they would never see the other side. When they were some distance out to sea, the ships were stopped, and their crews started seizing the women and children. Their screams echoed out across the frigid water, chilling the bones of all those who watched in dread from the shore, as they were cast into the sea. Their shrieks turned to gasps then to splutters and coughs as the icy sea began to overwhelm them. Some of the stronger ones tried to swim and clawed at the flanks of the great ships screaming for help or mercy, ripping out their fingernails trying to make their way back on the ships. But the crews just laughed, grabbed the children, and threw them overboard. Some of the desperate women must have tried to save those children; others, drowning, panicking, must have seized their fellow Armenians and dragged them under in their dying terror. The cold water was quick to paralyze many of them. Their shrieks reached a climax when the crews had thrown most of them into the water and started sailing back, leaving them thrashing and floundering with no hope of making it to the shore. But as they drowned in the thousands, the eerie screaming that echoed across the Black Sea's waves diminished. Eventually, the last set of waving arms above the water became still, and the last desperate, thrashing woman was overwhelmed by the waves. Silence fell, and the silence was infinitely worse than the screaming.

* * * *

While many of those who witnessed the atrocities in Trebizond simply remained silent, complicit in the genocide by their unwillingness to speak against it—or perhaps terrified into silence by the fear that something similar would happen to them—these events are known to history because of a courageous handful of Ottoman citizens who were brave enough to testify against those who perpetrated these unspeakable crimes. Among them were doctors at the hospital who had to watch in disgust as their colleagues killed innocent children, foreign ambassadors, and even members of the government who were unable to stop the killing but would later appear in court to tell of the terrible things that had happened. Most of these would testify years after the end of the First World War. But one small group of people was feeding information constantly to the British, telling them about the Ottomans' plans, about the killing of the Armenians and other minority groups. And Eitan Belkind was among them.

The truth was that while almost everyone thought he was simply a harmless agronomist seeking to save Ottoman crops from the ravaging locusts, nothing could be further from the truth. Eitan had always had a fire inside him, a desire to see justice done for his fellow Jews and other minorities. And that fire caused him to co-found, alongside his friend Aaron Aaronsohn, a secret organization known as NILI.

NILI was an acronym for "Netzah Yisrael Lo Yeshaker," Hebrew for "The Eternal One of Israel will not lie," and it was a Jewish spy ring that worked for the British in a bid to bring down the Ottoman Empire. Israel, the homeland of the Jewish people, had been under Ottoman occupation for four hundred years; now, the much-oppressed Jews were being deported from their ancient homeland just like the Armenians, and Aaron and Eitan were determined to make it stop. The simplest way to do so would be to get the British who were based in Egypt to invade the Ottoman Empire and liberate Israel. For years, Aaron, Eitan, and their fellow NILI spies had been traveling across the empire under the pretense of being government agronomists, gathering information to help the Ottomans' enemies.

It was a homing pigeon that eventually brought down NILI in late 1917, more than a year after the mass drownings at Trebizond. It landed on the wrong rooftop, and the Turkish governor who lived in the home was able to crack the code in the encrypted message it carried. The NILI members were rounded up, jailed, and sentenced to death. But while they languished in jail, in December 1917, the British used the information that NILI had provided to invade Palestine and take back Jerusalem, liberating it from four centuries of Ottoman rule. As for Eitan, he and some of his fellow NILI members were able to escape from jail as the Turks fled from the advancing British. Eitan's testimony about the Armenians became a key part of allowing the world to know what had really happened and of finding justice for the perpetrators. With his work done, Eitan was able to live out his life as a peaceful agronomist (for real this time), and he died in 1979 having lived a long and full life.

But by the time the British took Palestine, it was, of course, far too late for the Armenians. Back at the start of 1916, they were still being butchered by the hundreds. And it would be a long time before their suffering would finally be at an end.

Chapter 10 – Stolen Children

The more Armenian men and women that they killed, the larger a single problem grew for the Ottoman Empire: what to do with the orphans that remained.

Azmi, of course, had his own way of dealing with the children—namely, injecting them with deadly bacteria or giving them an opioid overdose, burning them, and throwing them into the Black Sea. However, none of those ways were really profitable. All the good Armenian plunder had already been taken by the time the terrified and helpless orphans were killed in the thousands. Azmi wanted more than just death; he wanted money and pleasure too, and like other perpetrators of the genocide, he would find both in the waves of orphans that came into Trebizond.

Perhaps one of the greatest atrocities that Azmi committed was to use the orphans as sex slaves—often ten or more at a time—and then have them killed afterward. His son likely did the same when Azmi picked out thirteen of the prettiest young Armenian girls and gave them to the young man as a gift. Tragically, this was not unusual, and orphans were not the only targets. Armenian women and children were stolen from their own families and sold off as sex slaves; girls were raped and then forced to join the harems of important and brutal Turkish men.

Not all of those abducted would be forced into sex slavery, however. Some would have a different core element of themselves taken away from them: the faith that they and their families had practiced for generations.

Sold or abducted into Muslim families, the Armenian women and children would be stripped of everything that their race had stood for since ancient times. They were forbidden to speak their own language or to worship according to their own beliefs; instead, they were held down as Islamic tattoos were forced onto their bodies. To many of them, who had been raised in a completely different religion, the experience must have been akin to rape—the rape of one's very soul. Forced into silence and threatened with death, they were made to practice a faith they did not believe in. Even worse, they must have been treated harshly, even though they had been forcibly "converted." They were little more than slaves in these Muslim households, and Armenian women who had been married off to Turkish men were forbidden to own any property.

Not all of the Armenian-Turkish marriages were things of grief and hatred, however. In fact, many Turks were determined to save as many Armenian women as they could by marrying them, which would make them off-limits to the marauding Ottoman soldiers. Eitan Belkind wrote of one Turkish man who had married five Armenian wives to save them from the genocide.

Some Armenian families were so desperate, faced with deportation and/or brutal execution, that they voluntarily gave up their children to their Muslim friends or neighbors—assuming they had any left that didn't want to kill them. Even though they knew their children would be raised as followers of Islam, at least they wouldn't be exiled and/or killed. Whether they had been abducted or voluntarily given up, many of these children were nonetheless mistreated, used simply for their labor and with many of the girls put into harems. They were forced to abandon their faith and the language they'd been born into, and the national identity that the Armenians had been clinging to for so many years was quietly wiped away. Their very culture was in danger of annihilation.

After the genocide, rescue missions would reveal the atrocities that these enslaved women and children had to endure at the hands of their brutal masters. Some men had vast numbers of sex slaves at their command; one record states of a Muslim man who "owned" twelve underage Armenian girls. Their rescuers could only get them back by buying them, as if they were sheep or cattle.

Children, women, and lives were not the only things that the Turks were taking from their Armenian neighbors, however. Armenians had wealth and property too—and many greedy Turks were determined to get their hands on it.

* * * *

Ahmed Riza could not believe his ears.

A fiercely handsome man in his sixties, Ahmed Riza was a man of many talents. A scientist, mathematician, and proficient politician, he had joined the Young Turk Revolution and become one of the most prominent members of the CUP. At the time of the First World War, the President of the Senate was only one of his many titles, and he was intimately involved in the workings of Parliament.

Ahmed Riza had seen a lot of trouble in his time. He had been a witness to the Armenian massacres in the preceding years, and even now, he was well aware of the deportations that were occurring throughout the empire. Unlike most representatives of Parliament, however, Ahmed Riza was not comfortable with the deportation of the Armenians. And now he could not believe what the CUP's Central Committee was saying.

When the Armenians were first deported, they had been given ten days to carry out an ultimatum imposed upon them by the Ottoman government—an ultimatum that may have even brought a flicker of hope to the victims of the deportations. They were told to close up their homes and businesses exactly as they were, taking nothing and certainly selling nothing; their money was all to be deposited into the bank under the name of friends or relatives from abroad, and they were to leave behind all of their possessions. Livestock and buildings, fields and crops, equipment and machinery, furniture and appliances, cups and plates and forks, beds and pillows and pets— they were all to be left just as they were. The Ottoman government assured the Armenians that this would be so that everything could be preserved exactly as it was for their eventual return to their homes once the war was over. Perhaps the Armenians felt a stirring of hope and comfort at the thought of leaving everything as it was. Perhaps they believed that they would be returning to the lives they had built for themselves in the empire that didn't want them.

Or perhaps they were already suspicious. Perhaps they already knew what was coming.

By September 1915, vast numbers of Armenians had been murdered or exiled, and the towns and villages were filled with shops and houses whose empty windows stared out onto the street like the dead eyes of their former owners left in the desert. The sheer amount of property and capital that had been left behind was simply overwhelming, and the Ottoman government, now knowing that those Armenians were never coming back, was able to implement a scheme that may have been in play since the beginning, a scheme to give the Armenians' considerable wealth to new, Muslim owners. This may have been part of the motivation for the Armenian Genocide from the very beginning, and now it came to its dreadful fruition as the CUP passed the Temporary Law of Expropriation and Confiscation. This law was better known by its sickly euphemism, the "Abandoned Properties" law. Its decree was simple and awful: all properties owned by dead or deported Armenians would immediately be confiscated and become the property of the Ottoman government.

Ahmed Riza was utterly appalled. He knew that naming it the Abandoned Properties Law was simply inaccurate. These properties had not been abandoned, he argued; they had been left behind when their owners were forcibly cast out of their homes and businesses and forced to walk hundreds of miles across the desert to their deaths. Despite the controversy that would undoubtedly surround his support of the hated Armenians, Ahmed Riza was loud in his opposition of the law.

"[The Armenians] were forcibly, compulsorily removed from their domiciles and exiled!" he protested. "Now the government through its efforts is selling their goods…This is atrocious! Grab my arm, eject me from my village, then sell my goods and properties? Such a thing can never be permissible. Neither the conscience of the Ottomans nor the law can allow it."

Ahmed Riza's loud argument was well substantiated too. He drew on articles of the constitution to prove why it was unlawful for the Abandoned Properties Law to be passed, but it was all to no avail. The single parliamentary champion of the victims of the genocide had vastly overestimated both the Ottoman conscience and the willingness of the CUP to adhere to the law. The Abandoned Properties Law was passed, and all Armenian assets were immediately seized by the government.

Some of these Armenian properties were sold off to Muslim Turks, often at a tiny fraction of their worth. Others were expropriated for warfare and poured into the slowly failing effort of the Central Powers to stand against the Allies. Either way, they would never be returned to the Armenians who were still alive. The Turks made their best effort to erase every trace of the Armenian culture from their towns and villages, making it feel as though the people had not only been destroyed but also forgotten.

Just as the savage guards had stripped the Armenian corpses of their clothes and left the dead men, women, and children naked in the dunes and gutters during the death march, the Armenian government had now torn away everything that the Armenians owned. And to this day, that property has not been returned to the families of its rightful owners. The vice president of Turkey lives in a mansion that once belonged to a wealthy Armenian, Ohannes Kasabian. Kasabian had the money to flee from the genocide and survive its wrath, but upon his return, he found that the stately home where he had once lived in tranquil prosperity had been confiscated. He would never live in his own house again. And until 2018, the leaders of Turkey had made it their official residence. Their equivalent of the White House was built on stolen ground. And after the genocide, the Turkish nation was rebuilt after the First World War on the lands of the Armenians that it had annihilated.

* * * *

To this day, reparations for the genocide have largely not been made to the descendants of the Armenians that survived it. The property confiscated by the Turkish government—the value of which today would be more than three hundred billion U.S. dollars—has remained in the clutches of those who took it, and the Armenians had to start over from scratch, even though they once made up a large proportion of the Ottoman middle class. In some ways, justice has still not been served.

But after years of relentless killings, the Armenians would start to see the light at the end of the tunnel. The destruction of their people was part of the death throes of an empire that was about to be destroyed itself. Relief was coming, but for millions of Armenians, that relief would be too late.

Chapter 11 – Justice

Fall had come gently to the Greek island of Lemnos. Admiral Arthur Gough-Calthorpe, standing on the deck of the British warship *Agamemnon*, couldn't help but admire the deep blue tinge of the water in the port of Mudros. The balmy October sun was still much warmer than he was used to back in England, but he knew that in summer the sun burned with a savagery that the pale-skinned British were wholly unprepared for.

The day was October 30th, 1918, and Calthorpe couldn't help but think back to this time three years earlier when hundreds of thousands of British soldiers were about to enter a bitter winter on the rocky peninsula of Gallipoli, Greece. They had used Lemnos as a staging ground for the invasion of Gallipoli, full of hope that taking the Dardanelles Strait would allow the British, French, and Australian troops to meet up with their Russian allies in the Black Sea, cutting Turkey in half and allowing the Allies to destroy the Ottoman resistance. Yet Gallipoli had proven to be one of the harshest front lines of the entire war—and one of the most humiliating defeats suffered by the British during the First World War.

Winston Churchill had been just a Lord Admiral then, and Gallipoli became known as one of his greatest blunders. Calthorpe could not have known that Churchill would someday become the prime minister who led Britain through a war even greater than the one in which Calthorpe was fighting right now; back in 1918, a war bigger than the so-called Great War was practically incomprehensible. Yet Calthorpe could feel the sense of relief that was starting to spread across the world for the first time in four years of utterly brutal warfare. The war was ending, and the Allies were coming out on top.

That was why Calthorpe had chosen to anchor the *Agamemnon* in the waters of Lemnos. It was a kind of symbolism to show the Turks how far the British had come since the disaster that had been Gallipoli in 1915. Plagued by heat, flies, dysentery, difficult terrain, and the appallingly unhygienic conditions, almost a quarter of a million Allied soldiers had become casualties of the Gallipoli front. They had taken the same number of Turks with them, but nonetheless, the British had had no choice but to evacuate in January of 1916. Yet that had not been the end of the British invasion of the Ottoman Empire's domains. Forcing their way through the Middle East—aided by Eitan Belkind and other members of NILI—the British had claimed many of the empire's Arab territories. By October 30th, 1918, the once-mighty Ottoman Empire had been brought to its knees. One cannot help but speculate on how things may have been different for the empire if it had concentrated more of its money and manpower on fighting the war with its enemies rather than butchering its innocents.

Now, Admiral Arthur Calthorpe was only a few minutes away from signing the Mudros Armistice with Turkish Minister of the Navy Rauf Orbay. He had taken Djemal Pasha's place as minister when Djemal had fled to Germany, knowing that he had committed more crimes than simply fighting his enemies in the war. He was guilty of much more than that.

He was guilty of genocide. And he would be condemned for it.

* * * *

Less than two weeks after the signing of the Mudros Armistice, which acknowledged the Ottoman defeat and their surrender to the British Empire, Germany also signed an armistice with the Allies on November 11th, 1918. A ceasefire was called, and the ugly mess that had been the First World War at last ground to a halt.

The aftermath was almost unthinkable, not least within the Ottoman Empire. As the Allies started to move through the empire, they were appalled that the reports of what was being done to the Armenians had all been true. The Mudros Armistice had forced the Ottomans to hand over all the surviving Armenian prisoners to the Allies; the stories they told were horrific, and the fact that there were so few of them was more horrific still. Before the First World War, two million Armenians had made their homes in the Ottoman Empire. By the end of it, when the genocide finally ceased, there were only about 400,000 left. Around one and a half million Armenians had died.

Clearly, something would have to be done. The people who had committed these atrocious crimes would be brought to justice, and so, a series of trials began in order to find and punish the perpetrators of the genocide.

The Allies had ordered Sultan Mehmed VI, who was (to his surprise) still on the throne, to organize courts-martial for the leading members of the CUP. They would be tried for entering the First World War on the side of the Central Powers but also for crimes against humanity committed in the form of the Armenian Genocide. Of course, the three people that the Allies were really after were not in the Ottoman Empire at the time. The Three Pashas had fled to Germany before the war ended, abandoning the empire they had so thoroughly desecrated.

While some of the trials were held in Trebizond—the city that had witnessed the gruesome mass drownings in the Black Sea—others were held in Constantinople. The fact that the Three Pashas were not present to be tried was not enough to stop the Allies from trying. They were tried in absentia at Constantinople in July 1919.

At the time, after years of turmoil and warfare, the Ottomans were a crushed and broken-spirited people. The rest of the world was appalled at the atrocities that the Ottomans had committed, and finally, the greater Turkish population of the empire was confronted with the blood that was on their hands. And while it was mainly soldiers who had done the killing, a truly tragic number of civilians had taken part too. They had formed gangs to oust the Armenians from their homes, and the more criminal elements had taken to killing, raping, and looting. Turks had adopted children whose parents had been slaughtered; they had bought the sex slaves that were a lucrative byproduct of the genocide. And even those who had not been directly involved in the genocide were living in Armenian houses and running businesses taken from the hands of dead men and women. And now that it was all over, the Turks became suddenly and terribly aware of what their people had done.

A pang of collective guilt flooded across the nation, filling the hearts and minds of the Turkish people. While the aftermath of the genocide could not be exactly termed as mourning, it was undoubtedly true that the Turks became aware of how terrible the treatment of the Armenians truly had been. Some of this guilt even made its way into the government. Spurred on by the Allied administration that was keeping a close eye on the proceedings, the court dealt ruthlessly with the cases of the Three Pashas. All three of them were condemned to death, the CUP was dissolved, and the properties of its members were confiscated by the state. In fact, these trials were the first time that the concept of a crime against humanity was introduced.

Sadly, however, as 1919 turned into 1920, it became evident that the early zeal of the Turkish court was starting to lose its fervor. Sultan Mehmed VI was too nervous to prosecute the powerful Young Turks; they had exerted a reign of terror over him as well as over the people, and where a strong sultan might have led the Ottoman

73

Empire forth into the light of day, their ruler failed them by cowering in terror, fearing a revolution. More than 130 high-ranking government officials had been arrested for the trials, and yet the sentencing was not taking place the way it was supposed to. The British intervened when little had been done by May 1920 and moved the proceedings to the more neutral ground of Malta, where it was expected that the Allies would deliver swift justice to the guilty. But it was not to be. The Turkish courts, possibly on purpose, had so befuddled the case and bungled the necessary documents that the trials could not proceed. Only a handful of the vast numbers of guilty administrators were ever sentenced, and no reparations would ever be made to the Armenian people from whom everything had been taken, even though originally the Allies had attempted to force the Ottoman Empire to give Armenia its independence.

The revolution that had so crippled Mehmed's resolve took place after all. In 1921, as the Malta tribunals were wading forth through a quagmire of red tape and messy laws, Mustafa Kemal Atatürk turned his slow-growing nationalist revolution into a direct threat to the British. He took a group of British people hostage, demanding that the political prisoners being held for the tribunals should be freed. Winston Churchill, at that time the secretary of war, had bigger problems on his hands than the mess of the Ottoman Empire. He let the prisoners go and left the Ottoman Empire at the mercy of Atatürk. Atatürk had none. Finding support in Soviet Russia, he launched a violent military struggle against the leadership of the empire, seeking his own power. Those Armenians that remained— some of whom had not been deported during the genocide—armed themselves and attempted to stand against him. They were crushed and massacred in what became known as the Turkish-Armenian War of 1920, adding thousands more to the death toll.

When the British withdrew from the Ottoman Empire, Atatürk picked up right where the Three Pashas left off. Atatürk was elected president of the new Republic of Turkey—the Ottoman Empire, by this time, had been dissolved—and he started deporting more and more Armenians again. However, this time, there was no real religious motivation behind their deportations. Atatürk transformed Turkey into a secular country, closing the Islamic schools and organizations and forming the new republic into something far more modern than the carcass of the Ottoman Empire from which it risen.

As for the Armenians, they would continue to suffer until 1923. By then, there were hardly any of them left to kill, and the genocide tapered off as the Republic of Turkey started to find its feet.

In the wake of the genocide, the Armenians started to find their feet once again, trying to put together their lives even after everything they once had was taken away from them. And the thing they wanted back the most may just have been their children. The children who had been kidnapped and assimilated into Muslim households were still out there, some of them having almost forgotten their Armenian identity (it had, after all, been eight years since the killing started). But others were being held against their will, wanting to get back to their homes and families.

Only a few hundred thousand Armenians remained in Turkey; most of them had fled to other countries and formed diaspora communities there, where, despite the suffering they had endured because of it, they continued to practice their ways and live in their culture. Their national identity had not been crushed by the genocide.

It had only been strengthened.

Chapter 12 – Operation Nemesis

Illustration IV: Armin T. Wegner in 1916

It had been a long time since the Armenians had really had a hero. Ali Bey, protecting thousands of refugees in Syria, had come close; so had Eitan Belkind, who fed information to the Allies, and Armin

T. Wegner, who helped to document the atrocities. But the next heroes who would rise up in the aftermath of the unthinkable genocide were not Arabic, Jewish, German. They were Armenian themselves, and they were seeking justice after witnessing the heartless desecration of their people.

One of them was Ruben Heryan. Having emigrated to the United States as a young man, Ruben could have done what thousands of Armenian Americans—and other foreigners —did about the genocide: sit back and shake their head grimly at the grisly articles in the *New York Times* or maybe donate a little extra money to the "poor starving children in Armenia." Ruben was well-off, well-respected, and well-liked in the community; there was no way that the genocide of his people could have caused him direct danger where he lived in New York. But he could not watch them die. By 1918, while the war was still raging, he had gathered a group of volunteers to join the Armenian Legion, a legion within the French Army, and made his way into the heart of the Ottoman Empire. His mission was simple: rescue.

It proved not to be as simple as Ruben had hoped. 1918 was a frustrating year for him. He was in his fifties already, and although his cheerful demeanor and can-do attitude had earned him the nickname of "the young man with the gray hair," he was no longer capable of fighting on the front lines. While his younger fellow volunteers were sent to the front lines, Ruben was stuck in Cairo, guarding a hospital. Perhaps it was in the hospital that he found his true passion, serving and saving the helpless. His heart was turned toward those Armenians who had been kidnapped into families they didn't know and forced to be someone that they weren't. He thought of the women and children who had been abducted or sold into Muslim homes, and he was determined to get them back.

Once the Three Pashas had fled the empire, Ruben was able to launch his rescue mission in earnest. Traveling the length and breadth of the empire from Deir ez-Zor to Constantinople, he started to raise funds in order to save the kidnapped Armenians. His heartfelt account of the generosity of his own people evokes both pity and respect; while the wealthy Armenians who had escaped the genocide were able to give sizable donations, some of the money that Ruben managed to raise came from utterly penniless victims of the genocide. They were still leaving the concentration camps, riddled with lice, sick, skeletal, and with only a couple of coins to their name. But when they heard of the women and children being held by the Muslims, they felt that these strangers' plights were worst and so gave their last scraps of money to Ruben and his team.

Every penny they could collect was desperately needed. The Muslims would not give up their Armenian captives easily; they hid their identities or smuggled them out to secret locations, making the searches almost impossible in many instances. Ruben spent months, sometimes years, seeking for specific women or children. Once they were found, almost the only way to get them back was to buy them. The whole operation was costly in terms of finances, but it was even more costly in emotional terms. Ruben brokenly described how some of the captives he discovered had seemed to have forgotten who they really were. Fully grown women, who could no longer speak Armenian, had wiped away the traces of their ethnicity in a bid to survive. Children who could not remember their real parents clung to their Muslim adopters. There were sex slaves who were too frightened to speak up for themselves or open up to their rescuers. Stockholm syndrome would inevitably have been a tragic part of Ruben's mission.

The genocide would end in a few years, but in many ways, it lived on forever in the minds of those it had so brutally afflicted. Komitas was one of them. Even though he had returned to Constantinople and did not have to suffer the horrors of the concentration camps at Deir ez-Zor, he would never recover from the post-traumatic stress disorder that the deportation and death marches had given him. He was shuttled from one psychiatric hospital to the other for the rest of his life until he died in 1935.

* * * *

Ruben Heryan was one of the very first heroes of the Armenian Genocide. He worked tirelessly to find, save, and protect captive Armenians in what became known as the Liberation Mission, giving them the chance to grow up the way they had been born: Armenian. He freed them from the often cruel and oppressive clutches of those who had bought or abducted them, and he gave them a chance to live a new and different life on their own terms.

Other Armenian heroes, however, would not be as gentle or devoted as Ruben was. Their mission would not be rescue. It would be justice, and if the rest of the world was not going to carry out the Three Pashas' death sentences, then one group of Armenians decided that it would have to be their duty.

The Armenian Revolutionary Federation, which had pledged its alliance to the CUP when it was first formed, had been thoroughly kicked in the teeth for its attempt to mend fences with the Turkish back in 1908 before the Young Turk Revolution. Many of its members had been among those intellectuals arrested on April 24th, 1915, the eve of the genocide. Others had escaped and survived, however, and the ARF had been responsible for the resistance that had sparked the Turkish-Armenian War in 1920.

Now that the wars were over, the ARF turned its focus to gaining justice after the genocide. It was decided that there was only one way to do this: to find and kill those who had perpetrated the genocide. A blacklist was made, 200 names long, of those who had been the guiltiest. Some of the most important of these were the Three Pashas and Cemal Azmi, the Butcher of Trebizond.

Shahan Natalie was the leader of the group, which dubbed themselves Operation Nemesis. From their headquarters in Watertown, Massachusetts, Nemesis started to put together a plan to eliminate the enemies of the Armenian people. And the most important of them all was Talaat Pasha. Talaat had been so deeply bent on destroying every living Armenian, innocent or not, that he had ordered Ali Suad Bey to kill 30,000 starving and terrified refugees. Talaat had wanted the entire nation dead, and now that nation demanded his death, too.

On March 15ᵗʰ, 1921, the death sentence that had been laid upon Talaat in 1918 was finally carried out but not by an executioner. Instead, it was done by a young, handsome, dark-eyed engineering student named Soghomon Tehlirian.

Like practically every surviving Armenian, Soghomon was haunted by the memories of his family and how they had died in the thoughtless brutality of the genocide. His mother, in particular, had been beheaded in the genocide. To make matters worse, Soghomon had epilepsy, and the fear of a seizure coming upon him at any moment had made life difficult from the start. Still, he wanted to move on with his life. He wanted to settle down and marry his girlfriend Anihad, whom he loved more than anything. Yet the memory of his family, the knowledge that they would never have the peaceful life that he could lead in the United States, was intolerable. He had to do something. He had to *kill* something; he had to take from someone what had been taken from him. So, when Shahan Natalie looked into his dark, turbulent eyes, he knew he was looking at someone whose love and agony could make them a deadly force to be reckoned with.

In 1921, Operation Nemesis flew Soghomon out to Berlin, where Talaat Pasha had been hiding for the three years since he had fled the Ottoman Empire. For months, deeply undercover and sharing a room with some students, Soghomon studied his neighbor across the street, Talaat Pasha, the man who had murdered three-quarters of the Armenian race. To all appearances, Talaat was no one of importance. He had grown out his beard, and he lived a quiet life between his two burly bodyguards, and he liked nothing more than taking a soothing morning stroll at precisely 11:00 a.m. in the park.

The stroll was his fatal mistake. Arming himself with a Luger pistol on a nippy spring morning, Soghomon quietly began to follow Talaat from his residence. It was all he could do to stay calm as he walked in the very footsteps of the man who had ordered the deaths of hundreds of thousands, of the man who had killed his mother. Soghomon had not been in Armenia during the genocide (despite what he would later say at his trial), but he did have one particularly vivid and painful memory from that period: he had joined the Russian army in the liberation of Van from its siege in 1915, and while with the army, he had come across a little girl running through the woods, crying relentlessly. When Soghomon grabbed her, he was shocked to recognize her pale, dirty face. It was his niece, Armenouhi. She had just witnessed the genocide.

It was the memory of his mother's smile, of Armenouhi's terrified cries, that spurred Soghomon to do what he did next. He took the pistol out of his coat and cried out one word. "Talaat!"

Talaat Pasha turned, a flash of fear crossing his face. Soghomon raised the pistol and gave Talaat what he had denied thousands of Armenians that were drowned or burned during the genocide: an instantaneous death. Blood sprayed from Talaat's neck, and he fell to the ground.

The crowd around Soghomon immediately started shrieking, the bodyguards rushing toward him. When Natalie had given Soghomon his orders, his words had been blunt: "You blow up the skull of the Number One nation-murderer and you don't try to flee," he had said. "You stand there, your foot on the corpse and surrender to the police."

Soghomon knew that a public trial was part of Operation Nemesis' plan to draw awareness to the genocide. In the face of the charging crowd, however, he tried to flee. He didn't get far. The mob pulled him down and started to pummel him, and Soghomon might not have made it out alive if the German police hadn't been able to rescue him. The German police arrested him and took him to jail, and so began one of the most sensational trials the world had yet seen at that point.

By 1921, even though the Armenian Genocide would not officially be over until about 1923, the world had moved on from worrying about the Armenians and had started worrying about the aftermath of the world war in general. The brutal trench warfare had had a devastating effect on the global psyche, and the whole world had been changed by the conflict. The Armenians had started to become yesterday's problem, and Operation Nemesis was determined to change that. Soghomon's trial was an integral part of that plan.

As Soghomon had committed the crime in Berlin, it was considered a German matter, and so, he was tried in a German court. This turned out to work in Soghomon's favor. Germany was starting to feel the guilt of being associated with the Ottoman Empire and not doing anything to stop the genocide, and Soghomon's testimony of what had been done to the Armenians not only captured the attention of the world, but it also touched the jurors' hearts profoundly. True to Operation Nemesis' goal of sensationalizing the genocide, Soghomon's testimony was wildly embellished, especially considering that he had not actually been a witness to the deaths of his family, but it could have easily been the tale of any young Armenian who had suffered at the hands of the Turks.

Soghomon also related how he had suffered numerous nervous breakdowns after the massacres, something that may well have been true and something that his defense attorney was quick to note. The most striking moment of the trial came when the judge turned to Soghomon—who was on the stand—just after the indictment was read and asked him for his answer to the indictment. Soghomon answered that his answer was negative.

"But, prior to this trial, you thought differently," said the judge. "You admitted that you had premeditated the act."

His defense attorney requested that the judge direct his next question to Soghomon. "Why do you consider yourself not guilty?" "Because my conscience is clear," he stated.

"Why is your conscience clear?" asked the judge.

"Because I have killed a man." Soghomon squared his shoulders. "But I am not a murderer."

After only a two day trial, the jury voted in agreement of Soghomon's statement. Armin T. Wegner was one of the witnesses testifying about the atrocities of the genocide, and his testimony was a key part of Soghomon's eventual acquittal. Despite abundant eyewitnesses and evidence that Soghomon had decided to shoot Talaat Pasha and done so with premeditated intent, he was acquitted of all crimes and allowed to go free; even his pistol was given back to him. Officially, he had been acquitted because of a plea of temporary insanity. But the whole world got the sense that the jury agreed with Soghomon that justice had been served. In the words of a *New York Times* headline, "They had to let him go."

Chapter 13 – Denial

Talaat Pasha was not the only victim of Operation Nemesis. The operation pledged to cleanse the world of the stain of those who had perpetrated the genocide, just as those perpetrators had "cleansed" the empire of one and a half million souls, and the group made good on its promise.

Berlin was the scene of another pair of grisly assassinations. One of the victims was the leader of the Special Organization and a founder of the CUP, Behaeddin Shakir; the other was Djemal Azmi, the man who had butchered thousands at Trebizond. In Tbilisi, Cemal Pasha—the second of the Three Pashas, the one who had overseen the death marches—was killed as well. With two of the Three Pashas dead, Operation Nemesis only had one left to deal with: Enver Pasha, the fanatically warlike ex-Minister of War. But it turned out that when it came to assassinating Enver, Nemesis had to get in line. Fellow Armenians, employed by the Soviet Cheka (secret police), beat them to it. And so, despite the fact that none of them would ever face an official executioner, all three of the Pashas eventually got the death sentence that was coming to them.

In total, during the two years of its existence, Operation Nemesis was responsible for the killing of seven condemned perpetrators of the genocide and three Armenian traitors who had led the Turks to the doorsteps of their own people. Turkey, then and now, portrayed Nemesis as a terrorist organization; considering the grief that Nemesis wrought on the families of the men it killed and that it denied the men their chance at redemption in the eyes of the world, Nemesis can hardly be considered as a heroic operation. Yet there was a sense of international relief that the Three Pashas were finally dead.

Nemesis was as short-lived as it was controversial. In 1922, facing pressure after Armenia fell under the control of the Soviet Union, Operation Nemesis was disbanded. It had achieved its primary goal, and its chilling reign over the lives of the men with blood on their hands had left many more men with blood on theirs. Mercifully, the circle of revenge and killing more or less ended there.

Soghomon, according to those who knew him, did not find true peace in killing Talaat. However, his relentless wanderings came to an end, and he was able to settle down and marry the girl that he loved so much. They settled in Yugoslavia, where, many years later, Soghomon eventually threw the gun that had killed Talaat Pasha into the Danube River. He died an old man with grandchildren, something that his decisions had denied Talaat.

* * * *

When it comes to the Armenian Genocide, denial seems to be the overarching theme.

Despite the world's initial horror at what was taking place in Armenia, the governments of various countries were slow to officially recognize what had truly happened, perhaps in light of Atatürk's rising power. In fact, there wasn't even a word for what the CUP had done to the Armenian race. "Massacre" or "nation-murder" were the terms that were used at the time, but "massacre" hardly seemed big enough to encompass the extermination of an entire race, and "nation-murder" felt clumsy. And so, the world stumbled around the terrible weight of the bloodstained elephant in the room that the genocide had become.

Meanwhile, the "war to end all wars" had not brought about the peace that the world so desperately needed. Instead, tensions only escalated. In 1939, just 21 years after the end of the First World War, conflict erupted across the entire world again. Soldiers from all over the world would be dragged into the various theaters of the Second World War, from Japan to South Africa, from the United States to Germany, from Australia to the ever-growing Soviet Union. And like the First World War, this would see a number of despotic rulers rise to power. Most infamous among them was Adolf Hitler.

Hitler was determined to do to Germany, which had been flailing under the punitive measures imposed by the Allies ever since the Treaty of Versailles, what the Three Pashas had tried to do to the Ottoman Empire: cleanse it. He wanted to wipe away everything that he didn't like, and the Pashas may as well have been his heroes. The Jews were the Armenians of Germany, and Hitler would launch, on an utterly terrifying scale, the same atrocities the Pashas had committed.

By this time, Armenia had faded from the consciousness of the world, and the fact that Turkey had rebuilt its entire economy on the property that had been stolen from dead or deported Armenians had been allowed to slip away quietly and without contest. In fact, Hitler himself, as he prepared to launch the Holocaust, used the forgetfulness of the global conscience to excuse away the terrible things he was about to do. "Who remembers Armenia?" he asked, implying that even though the genocide had taken place less than thirty years ago, it had already been forgotten by most of the world.

But not everyone had forgotten. Following in the footsteps of his compatriot Wegner, a German writer and activist named Raphael Lemkin would be the first to name the terrible things that he saw occurring in the world around him. Lemkin wrote about the things that had been done to the Armenians—first in the ordinary letters of the laws that had stripped them of their rights and then, brutally, in the savage treatment that had been inflicted upon them—and drew highly unpopular parallels between the massacres in Armenia and the Holocaust of the Jews. It was Lemkin who would give this atrocity a name. He called it "genocide," and the world would finally have something to define the awful killings of an entire race.

The very term "genocide" would prove as controversial as Lemkin's opinions of it. In Nazi Germany, to be vociferously in opposition to the Fatherland and its dictator was to court disaster. Armin Wegner had not allowed fear to silence him; in 1933, he had written an open angry letter to Hitler denouncing his treatment of the Jews, using the strong words, "There is no Fatherland without Justice!"

The Gestapo came for Wegner and tortured him, and the great activist would go on to suffer alongside those same Jews in those same concentration camps, witnessing the terrible treatment of them firsthand before he was released before WWII broke out and fled the country. But despite what had happened to Wegner, Lemkin would continue to protest that what had happened to the Armenians was wrong and what was happening to the Jews was even worse. With his life in peril, Lemkin succeeded in leaving Germany to work with Americans in Washington, D. C., in 1942. It was here that he wrote his *Axis Rule in Occupied Europe*, and the word "genocide" first entered the world's vocabulary.

It was a word that Lemkin would use to good effect, too. He worked closely on the Nuremberg trials, where he first heard that nearly fifty members of his immediate family had been killed in the genocide for which he was prosecuting the Germans (Lemkin himself was Jewish). Of course, many of the most important perpetrators of the Holocaust had committed suicide before the trials. Adolf Hitler, Heinrich Himmler, and Robert Ley were among them.

Once the Nuremberg trials were over, however, the word "genocide" could not be put to rest. The world began to wonder where else genocide had been committed, and Armenia was the most recent. Armenians themselves were quick to adopt the term and just as quick to demand justice for what had been done to them.

The United Nations followed in 1948, acknowledging that what had happened in Armenia was a crime against humanity, even though by then there was almost no one left to actually prosecute for it— Operation Nemesis had made sure of that. By 1985, the UN officially recognized the events in Armenia as a genocide. Much of this is due to lobbying by Cyprus; it had legally recognized the genocide by 1975, and in the modern day, actually denying the genocide is a crime in Cyprus. The very first country, however, to recognize the genocide was Uruguay, which has had an Armenian population since the early 19th century.

One by one, countries across the globe have followed in recognizing the suffering of the Armenian people. Argentina, Belgium, Canada, France, Greece, Lebanon, and Russia all recognized the genocide in the 1990s; Chile, Germany, Italy, Lithuania, the Netherlands, Poland, Slovakia, Switzerland, the Holy See, and Venezuela followed suit in the early 2000s. There are a few nations, however, that have not yet made their respect for the Armenians' suffering official. Among them are the United States (although 49 out of 50 states do recognize the genocide) and the United Kingdom. Both of these countries have likely done so out of fear of angering Turkey because, of course, no country is louder in denying that the genocide ever happened than Turkey itself.

A simple number easily summarizes Turkey's stance on the genocide: 300,000. This is the number of Armenians that Turkey officially recognizes as having been killed in the genocide. This more or less assumes that about one million Armenians simply disappeared into thin air during the First World War, considering that around two million Armenians lived in the Ottoman Empire before the war, and only about 400,000 were left afterward. Historians and genocide scholars are in agreement all over the world that the figure Turkey stands by is grossly inaccurate.

Another Turkish stance on the genocide is that it was justified by the acts of the Armenians during the First World War. While it is true that Armenian rebels betrayed the Ottomans to Russia, igniting a revolt that claimed Turkish lives, it is unlikely that the thousands of women and children thrown overboard in the Black Sea at the command of the Butcher of Trebizond were in any way involved with any kind of rebellion.

Turkey similarly denies the fact that Greeks and Assyrians, who also suffered the same awful mistreatment as the Armenians during the First World War, were victims of genocide during the Ottoman era. The "Turkification" that the Young Turks began more than a hundred years ago is still in force to the modern day. Motives for denying the genocide are likely rooted in fears that to recognize the genocide would mean making reparations to the descendants of its victims—and considering that much of the modern Turkish economy depends on the burgeoning middle class, that might be disastrous for the country. There were very few middle-class Turks before the genocide; much of today's middle class started out as menial laborers who rose in the social ranks because of buying cheap Armenian properties.

The Turkish denial of the Armenian Genocide is so severe that merely mentioning the genocide in Turkey is a crime. However, pressure from the rest of the world to mend fences with Armenia may be starting to nudge Turkey toward recognition of what its hulking ancestor, the Ottoman Empire, has done. There is hope that, someday, Turkey will be able to acknowledge its mistakes, enabling the Turks and the Armenians alive today to move forward.

Chapter 14 – Fighting for Freedom

Illustra tion V: Mount Ararat towers over the city of Yerevan, capital of modern-day Armenia

In the wake of World War I, the Ottoman Empire's collapse left a power vacuum in the territories it had once oppressed, and the Armenians were finally able to take advantage of that vacuum.

For centuries, Armenia was passed back and forth from one ambitious empire to the other. Rome, Persia, the Ottomans—they had all been controlling the little country and its people for generations upon generations. But the end of WWI saw independence being given to colonies all over the world, and

Armenia was no exception. Under pressure from the Allies and still focusing on bringing together the new Republic of Turkey, Atatürk had to watch as the borders of the once-great empire splintered. One of those splinters was formally established on May 28th, 1918, as the Republic of Armenia.

Those Armenians who had survived and stayed in their ancestral homeland could hardly believe it. They were free at last. No longer would they be harshly taxed simply because they worshiped differently; no longer would they face massacre after massacre. As the genocide still continued within the borders of Turkey, a great flight of refugees started to pour from Turkey into Armenia. While these refugees were grateful to have finally found a place that was supposed to be their safe home, things did not bode well for the new little republic. Most of its population was crippled by the terrible genocide that had just taken place. With three out of every four Armenians in the Ottoman Empire killed during the darkness of the preceding years, practically every Armenian had either witnessed these atrocities, suffered through some of them, or lost someone they loved to them. The genocide was all-encompassing; it affected everyone, and the nation was brokenhearted after seeing the wholesale destruction of its people.

Knowing this, multiple smaller countries—themselves fragments of the shattered empire—saw Armenia as a target. Only a few weeks after the Republic of Armenia was established, it found itself under fire from neighboring Georgia over provinces on the border. Georgia was surprised to see the vehemence with which the Armenians resisted any of their lands being taken. Their people had been robbed of too much and for far too long, and they fought back with a spirit that was surprising considering what they had just suffered.

Azerbaijan was another antagonist of Armenia's bid to carve out its independence. Closely allied with Turkey—its culture and religion mirroring its intimidating neighbor —Azerbaijan took advantage of the fact that Armenia's borders had not yet been officially drawn. It laid claim to several areas of Armenia, including the capital,

Yerevan, in the shadow of Mount Ararat. Despite British intervention, a diplomatic solution was never reached. Azerbaijan invaded the Armenian borders determined to claim the land it saw as belonging rightfully to the Azerbaijani, but its claim would never be successful. Once again, despite the horrors that they had just suffered, the Armenians pushed back. By 1920, the Azerbaijani had been chased back to their own country, and Armenia seemed to be finding its feet at last.

The Treaty of Sèvres was signed in August 1920 between the Allies and the Ottoman Empire. One of its conditions was to define the borders of Armenia and also for all of the involved parties to recognize it as a fully independent state. The Ottoman Empire begrudgingly did so under its last sultan, but its recognition of its most hated enemy would not last for very long. Only a month later, under Atatürk, Turkey invaded Armenia on a scale that even these spirited people could not stand against.

By November, two-thirds of Armenia was under Turkish control. And by December, that control had been transferred once again. Just as Armenia had fallen victim to the Roman Empire and to Alexander the Great, it was now wheat before the scythe of the world's newest rising empire, the Soviet Union. Armenia became the Armenian Soviet Socialist Republic, and it would remain under the control of the Soviets for the next seven decades.

When the USSR crumbled in 1991, Armenia found itself free at last, but like many countries that had been deeply dependent on the Soviet Union, it was mostly free to starve to death. Armenia had been so deeply dependent on the USSR, particularly for fuel, that its citizens found themselves practically without electricity. In fact, they had to survive on only four hours of power per day. In the cold mountains of Armenia, it wasn't enough; even almost thirty years later, the country is still trying to recover from the deforestation and overfishing that took place as a starving people tried to make their way through the winter.

But Armenians had seen worse than this. It was seventy years after the genocide had ended, yet the terrible events were still alive in memories and in the gaping holes that had been ripped in family trees. They survived the darkness and rebuilt their country practically from scratch, and Armenia was declared, once again, to be an independent republic. Its first democratic elections held on October 16th, 1991. Despite considerable corruption and natural disasters that rocked the country, Armenia entered the 21st century as a nation that was slowly rising from the ashes.

Rigged elections peppered the first few decades of Armenian independence. Perhaps the most corrupt of the Armenian presidents was Robert Kocharyan, the second president of Armenia. Kocharyan should never have been president in the first place; he had not been an Armenian citizen for long enough according to his own constitution. Nonetheless, he succeeded in rigging the election so that he could take power and become the president of Armenia in 1998.

Kocharyan's main rival, Karen Demirchyan, was more popular with the people. He held the role of Parliament Speaker during Kocharyan's presidency, and together with the prime minister, Vazgen Sargsyan, he worked to sideline Kocharyan from the political scene as much as possible. Within a year, Armenian politics were largely in the hands of Demirchyan and Sargsyan, with Kocharyan reduced to something of a figurehead.

Until one fateful day in October 1999, when both of Kocharyan's rivals would conveniently be removed from the scene entirely.

* * * *

Parliament was in session, and Kocharyan was getting tired of hearing the voices of his two rivals drone on and on. They had all but seized control of the country, pushing Kocharyan to the sidelines even though he held the title of president. Some would argue that in doing so, Demirchyan and Sargsyan were helping Armenia on the road to true democracy and independence as a nation that was still fumbling for footing after centuries of rule by one greedy empire after another. It certainly appears as though Sargsyan was not corrupt or at least not as corrupt as his counterpart, Kocharyan. And some would not argue. Some would just pick up AK-47s, walk into Parliament, and open fire.

On October 27th, 1999, five gunmen did exactly that. Led by a former ARF member, they stormed the National Assembly building armed with machine guns. Journalists and politicians scattered for cover among the benches in the parliamentary building as the men headed straight for their target: the prime minister, Vazgen Sargsyan. They raised their voices so that the journalists could hear every word of their exchange.

It was Nairi Hunanyan, the leader of the group, who approached Sargsyan first with a gun aimed for him and a slew of accusations. Hunanyan called Sargsyan corrupt and a profiteer. His words as he strode up to the prime minister were chilling.

"Enough of drinking our blood!" he cried, seized by the fervor of bloodlust and what he saw as patriotism.

Sargsyan's reply was unruffled by the barrel of the machine gun leveled at his chest. "Everything is being done for you," he said, "and the future of your children."

After that, Hunanyan let his bullets do the talking. He poured rounds into Sargsyan at point-blank range, killing him instantly, and his fellow terrorists opened fire. By the time the bullets had stopped flying, eight politicians were dead, Sargsyan and Demirchyan among them. President Robert Kocharyan, whom the terrorists identified as being the leader that Armenia truly needed, was untouched.

This and other facts—especially the four-year trial that followed the shootings, which were handled so lackadaisically that the Armenian public could not help but speculate whether the government was dragging its feet in a bid to hide something—would lead to Robert Kocharyan becoming the main suspect that the Armenian people believed had instigated the shootings. It had certainly strengthened his position in Parliament; for the next ten years, Kocharyan's authoritarian rule would see Armenia's slow side away from democracy and into just another state ruled by a selfish dictator. Armenians protested, of course. They had survived far too much to suffer oppression from one of their own. When Levon Ter-Petrosyan, who had been the first president of Armenia, announced his candidacy in the 2008 elections, the protests took a turn for the violent. Ter-Petrosyan had proven to be something of a dictator in his seven years as president from 1991 to 1998, and he was widely accused of having rigged the 1996 elections. Trying to avoid yet another rigged election, protesters in Yerevan turned violent and started looting and attacking authorities. While the police at first tried to break things up using non-lethal methods, the situation escalated, and the military was called into Yerevan. By the time the violence was over, ten protesters had been killed. Their supporters argued that the authorities had been looking for a reason to open fire on them.

Ter-Petrosyan did not win the elections; instead, Serzh Sargsyan became president, along with a slew of promises that he would be different. Over the next ten years, it became evident that Sargsyan had little intention of making good on his promises. Going directly against what he had said before his presidency, he made himself prime minister as well as the president in 2018, amassing a dangerous amount of power. In fact, the people feared that Sargsyan would be able to stay in power for life.

By 2018, a wave of revolution was sweeping across the Middle East, and discontent peaked in Armenia. Yet memories of the bloodshed in 2008 forced the people to reconsider their tactics. Looting and violence were not going to be the answer; instead, nationwide protests would have to be truly peaceful. And to achieve this, a politician named Nikol Pashinyan knew that the people needed a leader.

Pashinyan was a nobody, a journalist who led a puny opposition party that barely featured on the radar of the Armenian people. But the nation needed a leader, someone who was brave enough to walk forward into the future, and at the end of March 2018, Pashinyan became that person. He announced that he was going to walk the 120 miles from the city of Gyumri to Yerevan, peacefully protesting Sergsyan's new appointment as prime minister.

When he set out from Gyumri, a handful of curious journalists were trailing after him. But when he reached Yerevan more than two weeks later, the streets were flooded with crowds of Armenians. They had painted faces and carried Armenian flags; they were laughing and shouting and cheering their slogans, and they had rallied around an ordinary-looking middle-aged man in a khaki shirt and cap. Pashinyan proceeded to lead what is now known as the "Velvet Revolution," an entirely peaceful protest and general strike that resulted in no deaths. The streets were closed, workers went on strike, but there were no casualties. There was no violence. Photographs show children on their parents' shoulders, holding up the flag of their people. In fact, it was downright civilized; Pashinyan asked his protesters to get off the street by ten in the evening. It was a protest with a bedtime.

When Sargsyan tried to get the army involved, even that failed. The soldiers laid down their weapons and joined the protest, and Sargsyan knew that he had been beaten. He resigned his post on April 23rd, after having kept Pashinyan briefly in prison. A short while later, Pashinyan's party was elected, and he became the president of Armenia.

Today, Armenia keeps on taking small steps toward becoming a whole and hopeful nation. This is a nation that survived genocide yet staged a revolution without any violence and without any support from any of the "big brother" powers—like the E.U., the U.S., and Russia. Like its culture, like its religion, like its indomitable spirit, the Velvet Revolution was nothing if not one thing:

It was uniquely Armenian.

Conclusion

One hundred years ago, Armenia was a name on the lips and hearts of America. Children who wouldn't finish their food were told to eat up because there were starving children in Armenia; missionaries were sent there, and the well-meaning donated to ACASR's cause, as the genocide—even though it could not yet be called by that name—became the cause of the day.

Today, however, newspaper articles published for an American audience have to clarify where Armenia even is. Even in Hitler's time, the genocide had already been forgotten by the conscience of the world.

Armenians, however, do not forget—not in the spirit with which they continue to move forward within their own mother country, and not in the vibrant and thriving diaspora communities that popped up all over the world in the trembling wake of the genocide.

All over the world—from Australia to France to Brazil to the U.S. and back again—Armenians have made their homes in foreign countries, continuing with their lives after fleeing from the wrath of the Turks. These days, the firsthand accounts of the genocide are stories passed down from great-grandparents. But many parts of Armenian culture are still a part of the lives of those who escaped the genocide. Armenian Americans could visit France and find food being served there by people who look like them, food that their parents or grandparents might have cooked in their own homes. There seems to be a link running through all Armenians, regardless of where they come from, a mutual recognition of who they are despite what they have endured.

Eight million Armenians today live in the various diaspora communities, the largest of these being in the United States (specifically Los Angeles) and the Krasnodar region of Russia. The Ottoman attempt to exterminate the Armenians once and for all could not have failed more spectacularly, although many regions of ancient Armenia, which are now no longer part of the modern Republic of Armenia, are totally devoid of ethnic Armenians.

Yet even though Armenia continues to lobby for Turkish recognition of the genocide, many Armenians are ready to put the past behind them and stride into the future, bringing with them not the bitterness of what their ancestors endured but rather the fearless spirit that allowed them to survive. An Armenian-American photojournalist, Scout Tufankjian, who has devoted much of her life to photographing people in the various diaspora communities, said it best.

"We are so much more than the genocide. We have survived. And we have thrived."

Here's another book by Captivating History you might like

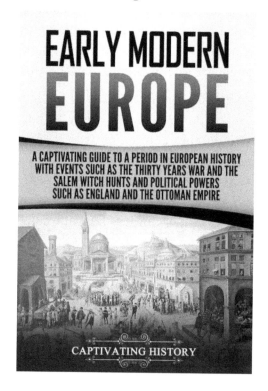

Sources

https://www.britannica.com/place/Armenia/The-marzpans

http://www.newadvent.org/cathen/07023a.htm

https://www.ancient.eu/Saint_Gregory_the_Illuminator/

https://www.plough.com/en/topics/culture/music/how-christianity-came-to-armenia

http://armeniancenters.com/armenian-history-summary/

https://www.thoughtco.com/timur-or-tamerlane-195675

https://greekcitytimes.com/2019/05/29/may-29-1453-the-fall-of-constantinople/

http://www.thenagain.info/WebChron/EastEurope/FallConstantin.html

https://www.britannica.com/event/Fall-of-Constantinople-1453

http://www.ottomansouvenir.com/more_on_ottoman_empire.htm

https://www.historyextra.com/period/medieval/6-things-you-probably-didnt-know-about-the-ottoman-empire/

https://www.history.com/topics/middle-east/ottoman-empire

https://www.huffpost.com/entry/the-armenian-question-a-s_b_185846?guccounter=1&guce_referrer=aHR0cHM6Ly93d3cuZ29vZ2xlLmNvbS8&guce_referrer_sig=AQAAAFqf_0Uld7R_ww1u-3zmtWUOsoPjAryYEpO2aC_4te3C9SFZBCyttdNx0_VwqqFGYGCk1vQZ2kezzQDqmyOxDP7Ndn51OQw7LN7qbdcaCpqVMxM_hsVTpQNqQ1bvMU2yn4ssVYWOo3fvR8UPP4eb93MTedg9J2Im-Zn6CCoyxSfE

http://www.arabnews.com/node/1487201/middle-east

https://www.newworldencyclopedia.org/entry/Abdul_Hamid_II

https://biography.yourdictionary.com/abdul-hamid-ii

https://www.britannica.com/topic/Hamidian-massacres

https://www.armenian-genocide.org/hamidian.html

https://journals.openedition.org/eac/1641

https://theamericanmag.com/queen-please-help/

https://www.geni.com/people/Rev-Crosby-Wheeler-D-D/6000000074716927124

http://www.hurriyetdailynews.com/opinion/william-armstrong/the-1909-massacres-of-armenians-in-adana-96825

https://www.armenian-genocide.org/adana.html

https://www.newworldencyclopedia.org/entry/Young_Turk_Revolution

https://ipfs.io/ipfs/QmXoypizjW3WknFiJnKLwHCnL72vedxjQkDDP1mXWo6uco/wiki/Ahmed_Niyazi_Bey.html

https://www.thoughtco.com/causes-that-led-to-world-war-i-105515

https://medium.com/@dhireshnathwani/what-was-the-most-significant-cause-of-world-war-one-ww1-74bb9e815e37

https://www.history.com/topics/world-war-i/world-war-i-history#section_2

http://www.thenagain.info/WebChron/EastEurope/TurkeyCentral.html

https://nzhistory.govt.nz/war/ottoman-empire/enters-the-war

https://www.britannica.com/topic/Balkan-Wars

https://www.hmd.org.uk/resource/24-april-1915-deportation-of-armenian-intellectuals/

https://www.cmi.no/news/1531-100-years-since-the-deportation

http://chilingirianquartet.co.uk/armenian-komitas-songs/

https://www.britannica.com/biography/Komitas

https://www.theguardian.com/music/2011/apr/21/komitas-vardapet-folk-music-armenia

https://www.allthelyrics.com/forum/showthread.php?t=50631

http://ww1blog.osborneink.com/?p=7328

https://www.historynet.com/the-defense-of-van.htm

https://www.armenian-genocide.org/wegnerbio.html

https://www.yadvashem.org/righteous/stories/wegner.html

http://100years100facts.com/facts/armin-wegner-took-pictures-saw-1915/

https://www.huffpost.com/entry/armenian-genocide-controversy_n_7121008

http://www.armin.am/armeniansgenocide/en/Encyclopedia_Of_armenian_genocide_death_march

https://encyclopedia.ushmm.org/content/en/article/the-armenian-genocide-1915-16-in-depth

https://www.irishtimes.com/culture/books/armin-wegner-the-german-who-stood-up-to-genocide-of-both-armenians-and-jews-1.2201998

http://www.genocide1915.org/bildgalleri_wegner.html

https://www.ushmm.org/information/exhibitions/online-exhibitions/special-focus/armenia/testimonies

https://qz.com/1310263/americas-extraordinary-history-with-armenian-refugees/

https://archive.nytimes.com/www.nytimes.com/ref/timestopics/topics_armeniangenocide.html?mcubz=0

https://books.google.co.za/books?id=h7ZIDwAAQBAJ&pg=PA205&lpg=PA205&dq=ali+suad+bey&source=bl&ots=NmgsuKPjkK&sig=ACfU3U2HqZIgVEq44BpBp1ctKP0RnXom2w&hl=en&sa=X&ved=2ahUKEwiLhbeSmbTkAhUEKewKHVOoAq8Q6AEwBnoECAgQAQ#v=onepage&q=ali%20suad%20bey&f=false

https://www.armenian-genocide.org/1915-3.html

https://www.quora.com/How-was-the-Armenian-Genocide-carried-out

https://books.google.co.za/books?id=McsxDwAAQBAJ&pg=PA655&lpg=PA655&dq=%22ali+suad+bey%22&source=bl&ots=vD6zZ2gmlh&sig=ACfU3U1tnCKZMsoAF1Clbyzv4GjR7tWOnA&hl=en&sa=X&ved=2ahUKEwjt49PUmbTkAhWGyKQKHXGKB9QQ6AEwBnoECAgQAQ#v=onepage&q=%22ali%20suad%20bey%22&f=false

https://www.catholiceducation.org/en/controversy/persecution/who-remembers-the-armenians.html

https://hyetert.org/2012/03/29/the-armenian-genocide-and-the-extraordinary-role-of-deir-zor-governor-zeki-bey/

https://www.armenian-history.com/Nyuter/HISTORY/ARMENIA20/armenian_genocide.htm

http://www.uacla.com/eitan-belkind.html

http://www.gen-mus.co.il/en/person/?id=2493

https://www.jewishvirtuallibrary.org/the-nili-spy-ring

https://www.medicinenet.com/typhus/article.htm

http://www.noravank.am/eng/issues/detail.php?ELEMENT_ID=371
8

https://armenianweekly.com/2016/05/31/ruben-heryan/

https://www.britannica.com/biography/Ahmed-Riza

http://100years100facts.com/facts/turkeys-economy-today-based-part-confiscated-armenian-property/

https://mirrorspectator.com/2018/04/19/commemorating-genocide-the-role-of-property-seizure-in-the-armenian-genocide-and-its-aftermath/

https://encyclopedia.ushmm.org/content/en/article/the-armenian-genocide-1915-16-overview

https://www.bbc.co.uk/bitesize/articles/zkb86v4

https://www.history.com/this-day-in-history/world-war-i-ends

https://www.history.com/topics/middle-east/ottoman-empire#section_9

https://nzhistory.govt.nz/war/ottoman-empire/at-war

https://www.volkansadventures.com/history/turkey-first-world-war-armistice-mudros/

https://www.dailysabah.com/feature/2018/10/30/the-armistice-that-spelled-the-end-of-the-ottoman-empire

https://www.iwm.org.uk/history/9-reasons-why-gallipoli-was-one-of-the-worst-fighting-fronts-of-the-first-world-war

https://www.history.com/topics/world-war-i/battle-of-gallipoli-1

http://endgenocide.org/the-armenian-genocide-where-is-justice/

https://www.oxfordscholarship.com/view/10.1093/acprof:oso/97801
99671144.001.0001/acprof-9780199671144-chapter-4

https://ayfwest.org/news/the-constantinople-war-crimes-trials-the-legal-response-to-the-armenian-genocide/

https://www.history.com/topics/middle-east/kemal-ataturk#section_2

http://www.armeniapedia.org/wiki/The_Trial_of_Soghomon_Tehlirian

http://100years100facts.com/facts/talaat-pasha-assassinated-berlin-15th-march-1921/

https://www.independent.co.uk/voices/robert-fisk-armenian-genocide-conversation-son-of-soghomon-tehlirian-mehmet-talaat-pasha-a7091951.html

https://www.huffpost.com/entry/erics-bogosians-operation_b_7097268

https://www.spectator.co.uk/2015/06/the-long-shadow-of-genocide-armenias-vengeance-years/

https://www.telegraph.co.uk/news/worldnews/europe/turkey/11373115/Amal-Clooneys-latest-case-Why-Turkey-wont-talk-about-the-Armenian-genocide.html

https://eurasianet.org/turks-commemorate-armenian-genocide-despite-taboos

http://www.genocidewatch.org/aboutus/thecostofdenial.html

https://ahvalnews.com/armenian-genocide/turkey-pays-price-denying-armenian-genocide

https://encyclopedia.ushmm.org/content/en/article/international-military-tribunal-at-nuremberg

https://www.operationnemesis.com/

https://www.nytimes.com/2015/04/19/books/review/19bkr-kanon.t.html

https://www.history.com/topics/world-war-i/armenian-genocide

https://www.bbc.com/news/world-europe-43948181

https://www.thenation.com/article/armenia-revolution-elections/

https://narcokarabakh.net/en/profiles/rkocharyan

https://www.rferl.org/a/Ten_Years_Later_Deadly_Shooting_In_Arm
enian_Parliament_Still_Echoes/1862158.html

https://www.nytimes.com/2008/03/02/world/europe/02armenia.html

http://www.littlearmenia.com/html/little_armenia/armenian_history.
asp

https://www.advantour.com/armenia/history.htm

http://www.auschwitz.dk/holofaq.htm

https://www.dw.com/en/holocaust-remembrance-in-germany-a-
changing-culture/a-47203540

https://journals.openedition.org/eac/565?lang=en

https://www.rferl.org/a/armenia-society/26935197.html

https://www.ft.com/content/2e2f38b0-e7a1-11e8-8a85-04b8afea6ea3

Illustration I: By Jean-Joseph Benjamin-Constant - Art Renewal
Center Museum, image 10603., Public Domain,
https://commons.wikimedia.org/w/index.php?curid=1818511

Illustration II: By en: American Committee for Relief in the Near
East - from usa gov site. REPRODUCTION NUMBER: LC-DIG-
ggbain-27083 (digital file from original negative) RIGHTS
INFORMATION: No known restrictions on publication. MEDIUM:
1 negative : glass ; 5 x 7 in. or smaller., Public Domain,
https://commons.wikimedia.org/w/index.php?curid=9462125

Illustration III: By Henry Morgenthau - Ambassador Morgenthau's
Story Doubleday, Page p314,
(http://net.lib.byu.edu/estu/wwi/comment/morgenthau/images/Morge
n50.jpg), Public Domain,
https://commons.wikimedia.org/w/index.php?curid=3822803

Illustration IV: By Unknown - http://www.armin-t-wegner.de/biographie.htm, first published Im Hause der Glückseligkeit: Aufzeichn. aus d. Türkei (1920), Public Domain, https://commons.wikimedia.org/w/index.php?curid=30310497

Illustration V: By Hakob - en: Image: Yerevan_Mount_Ararat.jpg, Public Domain, https://commons.wikimedia.org/w/index.php?curid=1282772

CPSIA information can be obtained
at www.ICGtesting.com
Printed in the USA
LVHW081546220222
711727LV00004B/123